A SHARE OF LOVING

A SHARE
OF LOVING

Han Suyin

JONATHAN CAPE
THIRTY-TWO BEDFORD SQUARE
LONDON

First published 1987
Copyright © 1987 by Han Suyin

Jonathan Cape Ltd, 32 Bedford Square, London WC1B 3EL

British Library Cataloguing in Publication Data
Han, Suyin
A share of loving
1. Meninges————Tuberculosis
2. Tuberculosis————patients————biography
362.1′969958′100924   RC312.5.M45

ISBN 0 224 02429 9

Grateful acknowledgment is made for permission to reprint lyrics from
'Ballad of the Alamo' by Marty Robbins on p. 122. Copyright © 1960
CBS Robbins Catalog. All rights assigned to CBS Catalogue Partner-
ship. Reprinted by permission of Belwin Mills Music Limited, 250
Purley Way, Croydon, Surrey.

Phototypeset by Wyvern Typesetting Ltd, Bristol
Printed in Great Britain by
Butler & Tanner Ltd, Frome and London

A SHARE OF LOVING

To Bonnie
        Steve and
                Rich

Sincerely,

        Alan Snyer

March 1987

I

Writing about Peter hurts; he is too present, too much a part
of my life – or one of my lives. For, to be whole, I must
fragment myself; like a tree multiplying its skyward
gestures, I proliferate personae, and search my self-made
effigies in quest of coherence. And of this striving for
coherence Peter too is a part; hence I cannot file him away
into a dark corner of memory; into the labyrinth where all
passion vanishes as colour in the night of acceptance.

Peter adds a dimension to me, and to my life with his
father – my husband, Vincent. He also, of course, confines
us, tugging at us in that obsession which is natural to his
present state. Both a blessing and a blister; I sometimes
want to hit him. Hit a sick child, a boy of forty-three? His
father asserts that there has been great improvement; and
believes in the miracle-to-come. One day, suddenly, Peter
will 'be himself', coaxed back into the Peter we knew –
or thought we knew. I count the months, the years.
Sometimes I too believe that care, and loving, will break a
pattern with which I now identify Peter. For his mind does

grope; branches out, striving to re-establish an order of function. But it is *his* order, *his* way, not ours. It is characteristic of his affliction that he seems to model behaviour which will block off what one calls 'useful' activity and confirm a certain disarray of conduct which we now, at times, accept as 'Peter'.

'Do *something*, help me water the plants, Peter.'

'I won't, I won't.'

He walks off, jerking his hands, refusing to do anything which looks like 'work', which takes away from the lordliness which illness has conferred on him. This *appears* to me a deliberate, conscious refusal. It worries me, but not his father. 'He'll come round, give him time.' *Time.* It is precisely time that I am so short of.

Peter's behaviour seems wilfully prankish, for at times his brain is uncommonly clear. He pounces upon past memories, especially unpleasant ones, and dredges them up. He faces all of us, who care for him, with details of our lives, concealed items we choose to dismiss or ignore, censor out of ourselves. 'He loves to tease,' I am told. When he has made someone angry, or notices someone squirm, he is happy, shrieks with laughter, jerking his right hand convulsively, stamping his feet.

Perhaps there is truly Fate, Karma, Destiny, determining what happens to us. Belief in Karma makes the unbearable become bearable. So I too have my particular, determining rationale, explaining to myself that what has happened to Peter was due to something which took place in his childhood.

A warm November evening in Bangalore, that lovely city of South India, 1,000 metres above sea-level, where the summers are not torrid, the winters mild, and roses blossom all year round. Peter was there in the house he lived in as a child, the house Vincent had redesigned, beautiful and comfortable. I had come to spend two weeks with my husband, who now spent so many months in India away from me, caring for Peter, while I was in Switzerland.

Peter's brother, Michael, and his wife Anne lived permanently in the house, which Vincent had put in Michael's name; they had undertaken to help care for Peter.

We sat on the tiled verandah in the dusk, the scent of roses strong from the garden where Peter paced, striding among the flower beds. He spent many hours striding, arms flexed, hands tightly clenched, for he was in one of his active periods, which alternated with days of semi-torpor. Anne turned on the electric light, whisking back and forth in her elegant organdie sari. She taught by day in a school for mentally defective children, and took the task of caring for Peter seriously. Another servant (besides the cook, and the maid) had been hired to wash Peter's clothes. A second servant/bodyguard came by day, so that if Peter walked out of the house he could be brought back.

Anne whisked back from within the house, bearing three photograph albums. 'Have a look at these,' she said to me in that high, clear voice of hers, articulating each word with the detached mouthing of syllables characteristic of the Anglo-Indian.

The glossy plastic covers opened. Photographs. Of Vincent's three children, Michael, Peter, and Patricia, by his first marriage. Photographs, from babyhood in prams, through toddlerdom, to school shorts and braids for Patricia, and cricket for the boys. Vincent was nowhere in these photographs. 'I was away when the children were growing up,' he smiled. He was away, building roads in the Himalayan region of India. And afterwards he was with me, and only returned to India once or twice a year. Caro, his wife, was present. A neat, well-dressed woman, hair faultless (she went to the hairdresser once a week), her children around her, models of cleanliness and decorum.

Two pages full of Peter. Peter dressed as Little Lord Fauntleroy, with ruffled snow-white collar, long corkscrew curls. Peter, staring out from among those curls, a six-year-old Fauntleroy trying hard not to sob ...

'That was the way Mum dressed him. The boys all made

3

fun of him,' says Michael. Michael has told me that Mum loved his younger brother Peter, and Daddy loved Patricia. 'Why, Daddy even said he'd like to marry someone like her ... it hurt Mum,' says Michael. Nothing was left for Michael, or so he thinks. Perhaps he nurtures that feeling of being unloved, to explain his own life.

'Peter always won all the prizes ... ' Michael says. Peter is Little Lord Fauntleroy, good, perfect, faultless, and it is perfectly awful to note, in his six-year-old face, the distress. Anne laughs and calls out: 'Come, Peter, come and look at yourself ... '

'I won't, I won't.'

'You know,' Peter says to me, many years later, 'that is why ... that is why what happened, happened to me. Because they tried to turn me into something I wasn't ... that is why ... '

'Of course not, Peter,' I reply.

Peter paces the garden. He will always go away, and walk, walk, when someone comes near that part of himself he refuses to contemplate. Peter was the faultless one, with curls and snow-white collar, who never did anything wrong, and perhaps that is why, when he became so ill, he went on ignoring his own illness until he collapsed ... This is what I feel, deep within me. I say this to Vincent, and he replies: 'Don't make up things.' What use are explanations, trying to probe, to find out? Vincent smiles, a smile which says: You try to explain my son to me. I only go on caring, and believing.

'Oh, Master, time for your exercises,' Vincent calls out to his son, his son whom he drew out of a coma, calling to him many hours a day, many weeks, until one day, suddenly, he heard: 'Yes, Daddy.'

'Yes, Daddy,' says Peter, and stops pacing. He obeys Vincent, calls him 'Daddy'. Forty-three years old. He goes back into childhood, perfectly happy with Daddy. I have bought dumb-bells for Peter in the bazaar and make him do arm exercises, to unclench his fists, to move his arms. Later

4

I will bring those round balls of jade or steel which the Chinese roll round their palms, to keep the finger joints free from arthritis. I believe it is good physiotherapy for Peter's hands. I argue whether Peter is not taking too much medicine; I have seen reported somewhere that in America a certain drug given to schizophrenics has side-effects – it makes them keep their arms constantly above their heads. At night, Vincent will uncurl Peter from the clenched embryo position he assumes, his hands going over his son's muscles, making them relax, sending signals to the brain, through this touch of love, to let go, let go. And Peter straightens a little, lets go, says: 'I'm sleeping, Daddy.'

For thus it was decided when, in 1977, Evil struck at Peter – we would not institutionalize him. We would care for him. 'We' means, of course, the family, Vincent's Indian family. Taking it in turns to care for Peter.

'He'd die in an institution. He needs to be in the family,' says Vincent.

The family also includes me, and though I am not in the daily stint of caring for Peter, which Vincent has taken upon himself for several months each year, yet I too contribute. But this is not spoken about. No one starts counting what has been given to Peter, what is daily being given to him, in one way or another.

Sometimes I revolt against the whole set-up; I feel frustrated. For he is robbing me of Vincent, robbing me of time with Vincent, taking him away so much from me, from *us*, from the couple we are.

But there is the family. And I too belong to the family. I have to accept this other dimension, this other world, revolving round Peter – I have to accept or, at least, that part of myself which loves Vincent must accept Peter, as the family has accepted me.

II

In 1956 Vincent and I met and we fell in love. It was a passion both passionate and yet not for passion's sake. We were never tormented by doubt or uncertainty, though at the time everything seemed against us. Difficulties which we had to overcome we did, with a measure of insouciance, a lack of anxiety, a patience, which today seem to me rather extraordinary. We endured, waited for each other, as if space, distance, lack of communication, and time, did not matter. What mattered was that certainty of loving which was born in us and never faltered.

Vincent was in India, working as an engineer; I was in Malaya, running a medical clinic. Having met for a week in March of 1956, and having fallen in love, I immediately went off to China in April, for two months, leaving my clinic in the hands of a substitute. I was so certain that Vincent would be waiting for me, be there, when I returned to India. And he was. We met again for two weeks in late autumn. He knew how important it had been for me to return to China that year; I had not been back since the Revolution of 1949.

During the next four years I kept going to India once a year for a week, two weeks. I continued to run the clinic in Malaya, to go to China once a year, to take very brief trips in connection with my books to Europe and once to the United States. Truly a well-filled, busy life. I was solicited for seminars and international conferences; regarded both with awe (it seemed incredible, at the time, that I should go to 'Red' China and still remain so acceptable in anti-communist Malaya) and also with suspicion. But in the end I turned out to be right in my decision to let no barriers, no iron curtains (a favourite cliché of those unmellow years) stand in my way. And all the time, sustaining me, was that love between Vincent and myself – a love with a lot of physical distance between the lovers for most of the time.

By mid-1961, at last, geography no longer separated us. Vincent obtained a job in Singapore. We were able to live together, in my house, just across the Causeway separating Singapore from Malaya, in a charming town called Johor Bahru.

In our progress towards each other it was imperative that I should meet Vincent's family. Just as, later, Vincent would come to China and meet my relatives, my friends, and get to know my country. I, too, had to get to know his country. For one does not love or marry an isolated other; one marries echoes of parents, memories of squabbles with siblings, packages of reactions, habits, tastes, feelings, emotions, all bundled together to make a someone we love ... or think we love. Someone we think we know, and perhaps do not know, but constantly have to learn and relearn.

First of all I met Appa, Vincent's father.

It was in the winter of 1959-60. A winter etched in my memory, as it was in 1959 that the first friction between India and China over the demarcation of the border between the two countries began. I remember well how much I agonized over it. As for Vincent, he quietly resigned from the army (he was a colonel in the Madras Engineer Corps) and in that year began a job with a private company.

I went to China that autumn, returned briefly to Malaya (my patients were not always satisfied with my substitute and partners in the clinic) and then flew to India to see Prime Minister Nehru in December 1959. I had talked with Premier Zhou Enlai, and had suddenly decided – of my own accord – that I should go and talk with Nehru about the border problem which was producing such discord. The situation in Tibet had given rise to a wave of anti-Chinese articles. The flight of the Dalai Lama in that year led to a great many denunciations of Chinese policies. Yet it could be pointed out that, at any time during the seven weeks the Dalai Lama took to cross Tibet and to reach India, the Chinese armies could have stopped him ... and they did not. I wanted to talk over all these things with Nehru.

I did see Jawaharlal Nehru. Vincent, who came to Delhi to meet me and take me to Nehru's house, had arranged that we stay at the Asoka Hotel. Both Vincent and I were then asking our respective partners for a divorce, but it would be another four years before mine was accomplished, and another ten before Vincent's was also settled. We did not worry. Our discovery of each other was such joy that no amount of impedimenta could prevail. We had found each other. We had world enough and time, though time was but a few days, wrested from the passing months; we had total faith in the power of love.

'Appa wants you to come to lunch,' said Vincent.

'Your father? Why? Is he worried about us?'

'No, he just said: "Ask her to the house if she can spare the time." ' Vincent's talent for terseness is quite remarkable in a land where volubility is so common.

We flew from Delhi to Madras to have lunch with Appa the next day.

The house was on San Thomé Road, which is in the present suburb of Madras called Mylapore. Mylapore is a very old town, and a famous one. It was the birthplace of a Tamil poet and saint (of the Hindu religion, of course), Tiruvalluvar, who wrote the Tamil epic, the *Tirukkural*. Mylapore is today one of the most charming suburbs of that pleasant, widespread city. Running along its length is the famous Madras beach, some eight kilometres long, with its white-gold sand, its massive ocean waves, upon which dance the high-prowed fishing boats, crescent-shaped black and tan *masulas*, and the *catamarans*, those extraordinary vessels of logs tied together, swinging their 150-metre-long fishing nets. The Madras beach is the second longest in the world, and is a quarter-kilometre broad; the waters are reputed to be shark-infested and the undertow lethal, so that few people swim, except some valorous American youths I once saw emerge dripping from the tide. But in the mornings and evenings thousands of people stroll along the beach, and enjoy the turn of the wind.

Mylapore is also renowned for having been the site of the death of St Thomas the Apostle. St Thomas reached South India in A.D. 52, and here travelled and preached and made converts. It was on a small hill, now named St Thomas Mount, that he was speared to death (another legend says beheaded) in A.D. 68. For many centuries a church stood on the Mount, a landmark for mariners. The converts of St Thomas continued to cling to their faith, and this for all the centuries since his death. They were known as Nazarenes.

The Portuguese came in the early sixteenth century, and it is said that Vasco da Gama, in 1502, was met by a delegation of 30,000 Nazarenes when he landed in Cochin in South India. After that came attempts to unify the Latin Church of Rome and the Nazarene cults, now known as *syro-malabar*. Under pressure from Portuguese emissaries of the Pope, as the Portuguese now settled in the area, the Roman (or Latin) rites were introduced. But not all Nazarenes adhered to them. Some remained refractory even until this day, with their own bishops, priests and churches. Another faction, known as *syro-malenkar*, also

9

exists, and keeps to its own ways. Hence the Pope's visit to India, in February 1986, to reconcile these fractious Nazarenes with the Vatican.

The Portuguese settled where a small river, the Kum, formed a lagoon with low sandhills, and called their settlement San Thomé. Mylapore San Thomé became a fortified town of wealth and importance, essentially a Catholic town, with many churches (some of them, of delightful Portuguese sixteenth-century architecture, remain until today). The fortifications of the town were destroyed at the end of the seventeenth century by a Muslim army; then came the British East India Company. The British drove the Portuguese out, and built another fort, higher up the coast, called Fort St George; but they kept Mylapore and San Thomé, extending Madras to become a Presidency, a large area taking in much of what is now the Indian state of Tamil Nadu and two adjacent states. Throughout these conquests and shifts of power the area round San Thomé and Mylapore remained a Catholic stronghold. Later, due to British pressure, a number of the Portuguese and Catholic-Indian inhabitants settled further north, moving to Royapuram, up the coast, and to Tondiapet. In 1896 a large Catholic basilica was built on the site of what had once been a church on San Thomé Road, erected by the Portuguese in 1606. In its crypt lie the bones of St Thomas the Apostle. Here, it is said, he lived; from here he used to walk daily to the beach. The beach is just 100 metres from the basilica. St Thomas used to watch the fishermen bringing in their catch; they used the same *catamarans* that they use today. The Hindu scholar, K.N.Subramanian, in his book, *The Catholic Community of India*, writes that St Thomas may have met the poet Tiruvalluvar, who was of low caste, as his name indicates, because the *Tirukkural* in many respects astonishingly resembles the Sermon on the Mount.

Here, in Mylapore, Hindu customs and tradition intermingle with Catholicism. There is a statue of the Virgin Mary dating back to 1846. The cult of the Virgin has spread among the Hindus, so that they too go on pilgrimage to a shrine of the Blessed Mother, not far from Madras.

Mylapore also has Muslim enclaves, as well as Catholic churches, schools, colleges and convents. There are altogether only twelve million Catholics in India; Appa, Vincent's father, was the President of the Catholic Association of India. Appa's house stood on San Thomé Road, exactly opposite the Catholic cathedral. Like so much of the real estate in the area, it belonged to the Church.

Appa's house was old-fashioned, high-ceilinged, with the usual front verandah, red-tiled. We crossed the small garden shaded by a large rain tree. Appa stood up from the lounging chair in which he was reclining. He was fairly short; having shrunk with age, his trouser cuffs fell upon his feet. 'Welcome, welcome,' he said, and smiled at me. He had bright, lively eyes, a mop of white hair, and the nicest smile, unselfconscious, unforced. His eyes took in all of me, and did not reject anything. But as President of the Catholic Association of India, how could he condone his eldest son linking up with someone out of wedlock, someone who had rejected Catholicism?

Yet there occurred between us an immediacy of acceptance. Never, in all the years to come, would Appa ever query my ways of thought. Never did we speak of the pleasure we obtained in each other's company. All this was as it should be, so substantial as not to need words. Appa was the most reticent of men about his own personal needs or reactions. But he was a most eloquent speaker when he discoursed, at the Rajya Sabah (the equivalent of the British House of Lords) where he held a seat, on the misdeeds and defects of the Indian social structure. He lectured on law, and politics, at various universities; he also lectured on the exploited peasantry, the 'low caste', and then his eyes would flash, and his strong, measured words would roll forth in perfect English. For Appa had been educated in England at Jesus College, Oxford, from 1907-8, and then at Downing College, Cambridge, till 1910. He had then been called to the bar at Gray's Inn, and became a barrister-at-law in 1911. On returning to India he did not practise law, but instead took up teaching. Far less lucrative, but he was a man obsessed with the need to educate, which he did for the next fifty years.

The honours bestowed upon Appa were many. He became President of Madras Legislative Council and Vice-Chancellor of Annamalai University. He spoke English and French, knew German, Spanish and Hindi. Tamil, his own native language, he spoke but learnt to read and write only when he returned from England. Like Nehru, and many educated Indians of his generation, he had received in India a predominantly English education.

Appa had the reputation of being a fighter, and he was, on public platforms and in politics. But at home, he was all quietness. He carried silence tangibly with him, moved within an aura of non-noise. While his ebullient, noisy, turbulent four sons and five daughters would shout, laugh, quarrel around him, he appeared not to notice, absorbed in a book or in his thoughts. Sitting on the verandah, or disappearing into his study (not soundproof), he remained a presence. Appa. Perhaps ostensibly the least demanding of patriarchs, he was, actually, totally served by everyone around him. He never upbraided, bellowed or scolded, yet got everything done as he wished. When he was angry, he spoke in a very low voice, and his tall sons and daughters, planted around him, immobile, listened in silence, not even daring to wag their heads from side to side, in the Indian sign of acquiescence.

After Independence came to India in 1947, Appa was one of those who founded the Swatantra, or Freedom Party, a very conservative group. It was profoundly hostile to communism, and one of its members, Minoo Masani, would later distinguish himself in organizing some of the Asian intelligentsia in forums against communism, with considerable success in the West and very little in Asia. Swatantra has now disintegrated. Appa also founded the

Catholic Association of India; he promoted Jesuit educational institutions and is mentioned in Jesuit books. Catholic schools in India are still today reckoned among the very best. The affluent, the influential Hindu and Muslim families of India, will send their sons and daughters to Catholic schools, not to get converted, but to receive a good education. But Appa was also concerned to promote the welfare of the exploited peasantry, the untouchables, the tribal groups, the 280 or so minorities which in India are constantly subject to despoliation. His work and his speeches in the Rajya Sabah were devoted to what, in India, are euphemistically described as 'the weaker sections of society'.

Appa had been concerned, in the transfer of power from the British administration to the Indian one, to preserve what he considered was best: the parliamentary system and democracy. If he made mistakes, they were certainly not due to any political opportunism. And despite his profound Catholic convictions (he would go to Mass every morning, walking across the road to the cathedral), he now read Mao Zedong, and also Franz Fanon, whose book, *The Wretched of the Earth*, profoundly affected him and accompanied him on his many journeys by train throughout India. He could be described as one of those Catholics intensely concerned with true Catholicism: a religion which primarily took up the cause of the slaves, the defenceless, the poor ... until it became an institution dedicated also to its own power motivations.

In our first meeting, he asked me about Mao; about China, the communes, the Chinese Revolution. He had read my book on Malaya, and nodded slowly. 'You gave me a new understanding of the region. Please write some more books. We all have to learn ... to go on learning.' The shelves of the bookcases in his study sagged under the weight of books, books much handled, loved and pondered over. He spent whatever money he had (which was very little) on books, and he never had enough. He would go to the old

Connemara Library in Madras, with its stained-glass windows, its churchlike silence, and sit in the chairs in the front room, where a single fan relieved the summer heat without flurrying the leaves of the open volumes. There he would read, every Saturday morning, for some hours. When later I, too, went to the same library to consult old books in my search for the history of South India, Vincent would say, astonished: 'But you're doing just what Appa did! He used to go there. And a *peon* [servant] would carry a load of books for him, back to the house.'

He was astonished, because, of course, in their usual way of letting me find out everything for myself, neither Appa, nor anyone else, had ever told me of this habit of Appa's ...

After that first meeting, and lunch (Appa used knife and fork to eat his food, whereas his sons and daughters ate with their fingers, the Indian way), we said goodbye, Appa coming out on the verandah, and as we walked away Vincent said: 'Appa likes you.'

'I like him.' I did not say: You look remarkably like him, but you are not at all like him. Not at all. He and I are very much the same kind of people, though with very different ideas about the world. But you are, my darling, blessedly different.

This was my introduction to the Family. Vincent, being the eldest of the nine, then got me acquainted with his siblings. At first they were only names to me. Five sisters in gorgeous saris, three brothers, all tall, each one with a very different personality, but still elusive. All of them mad about cricket. Cricket, which I did not understand, would never understand, despite my own six years in England. Not a word about my being a 'lapsed' or 'renegade' Catholic. I had told them that, my mother being a Catholic, we had all been baptized, but something in me, very possibly the Chinese side, simply could not accommodate religion. I was a born Taoist, without knowing it. And my father – like all Chinese intellectuals, a man who considered all religions man-made – was a Taoist-Confucian

14

soul. He had deeply influenced me, without knowing it.

Never for an instant did anyone in that profoundly Catholic family comment on my own ideas. No one ever hinted disapproval because Vincent was trying to obtain a divorce from his wife and to marry a woman also in the throes of obtaining a divorce. This good manners, good breeding, which has nothing to do with money, or influence, was perhaps the reason why I realized that the world of the Family was a world of affection, of family links and loyalty, which had nothing to do with the outside world as we know it and live it.

On Sundays, whole rows of the benches in the cathedral were filled by the Family for, besides the nine, there were cousins, in-laws, second cousins, aunts and uncles, and children, down to the last baby. A contingent of forty to seventy would form the core of any family gathering for such occasions as festivals, pilgrimages, weddings, wedding anniversaries, birthday celebrations, special masses, memorial gatherings for the dead, funerals, and any and every other occasion which might present itself for getting together in rejoicing or mourning, or commemorating, or for greeting one of the Family back from 'out station' (an Indian term meaning somewhere else in India). There were also the Indian festivals and the Christian festivals – Christianity being so old in India, many Hindu customs were also incorporated in the tradition of Church celebration.

Very soon I was to find out that the real father figure, playing the father role, was Vincent, the eldest son, and not Appa. Appa was revered, totally listened to; but it was Vincent who was referred to for the settling of quarrels, the discussion of problems, the decisions about how to celebrate (very important, since each family gathering meant an outlay for eating – even the menu had to be approved by Vincent), the discussion of careers for off-spring, financial advice, how to get, from the pernickety and frightfully slow Indian bureaucracy, some action in the matter of housing, and a thousand other problems.

Appa, wisely, had totally detached himself, abstracted his spirit, from all such material details concerning his family. Everything, it seems to me, had been in the hands of his wife, Vincent's mother, Amma (whom I did not meet because she had died, in 1958, of cancer of the uterus). With the keys of the house tied in a corner of her sari, a tall, vigorous, beautiful woman with a great mass of hair – from the photographs – she had bustled from kitchen to living room, to the bedrooms, to the garden. She had gone on pilgrimages by train with all her brood, taking servants, a stove for cooking on, saucepans and brass pots for water. While Appa retired to his study to read, to write speeches, or went off to Delhi to attend the Rajya Sabah meetings, or travelled about lecturing, Amma ran the household. And Vincent, being the eldest son, had followed his mother about, and from her he had learnt how to cook. For cooking, the core and heart of providing for a family, is extremely important when one has to feed a crowd, not just an individual. I think he learnt from her how to deal with other human beings. He inherited, or picked up, this special gift of his: caring about people as they are, rather than about ideas, individuals, or 'humanity' at large. Whereas Appa and I were concerned with social causes, Amma and Vincent might have worried about a niece with mumps, a nephew with a hysterical wife on his hands. They would have made sure that these things were attended to. They would worry about a relative in Royapuram, who was going senile, and should have a servant to keep him clean. 'I really began to run the Family when I was round fifteen or sixteen,' Vincent says to me. 'I used to have to keep order in our crowd.'

And thus, while Appa remained free to pursue his studies, to disappear for days at a time lecturing on education or politics, Amma had looked after all things. Now Amma was dead. Appa was looked after by the two daughters who lived in his house. His sons, and other daughters, would

16

come to see him, at least two or three times a week. If they were 'out station', as soon as they returned they would come to visit Appa.

Thus, one by one, I came to know the Family. Cissy, the thin one, the most active of the lot. She wore my Chinese gowns, and we went to the races together, in Delhi. Louisa, round of face and large of body, looking astonishingly like her mother, Amma, and always talking about cooking, making one's mouth water with the way in which she described grinding the spices on the stone , chopping small the ginger and the garlic, and frying with *ghee* the lovely spinach and carrots fresh from the market. And fresh means morning-fresh, Louisa would reject anything that was over a day old. Any simple dish became, in her hands, a work of art; to be savoured and ooh-aahed over. Then there was Theresa, forceful, intelligent, who, had she not given up a career for matrimony and maternity, might have become a most successful businesswoman. There was Rina, tall, beautiful, with a trove of wit, a university degree, and now a housewife. And the youngest, Agnes or Aggie, beautiful, with the most lovely eyes and mouth, shy, and sweet-tempered. With loving, careful hands, and a silent watch-fulness, Aggie is not a modern woman. She is a giver. Gives devotion, care.

The brothers. Dominic, burly, assured, a successful army man. Basil, shy and quiet, masking his intelligence behind so much restraint, like his father. And Benny, who quarrels a lot with his sisters, but of course is also fond of them, and at times gives me the impression he is still, at around sixty, trying to find his own niche in the hierarchy of the brothers and sisters.

One of the Family's most endearing and infuriating traits is the way in which they are irrevocably, unhesitatingly, incessantly, always, always, *with* each other. Swimming in the same sea, as in a great womb, unalterably together. Even separated by distance, time, they write, write to each other. Vincent's family letters could fill up several boxes, did he not have the bad habit of tearing them up. Because, when one lives a situation considered so normal, one does not prize it. I rush to rescue them, but it is almost always too late.

Nine brothers and sisters, a solidarity organization, a tribe. There is for them, in each other's company, unending warmth, companionship, interest, continuous from childhood, continued until death, surpassing other relationships. Visiting each other, writing to each other, discussing all matters that happen to them, quarrelling with each other, taking sides, and then changing sides, then calling on Vincent, because he is the Eldest Son, to arbitrate – even today, when there is a quarrel brewing, we are kept informed by letter, all the way from Madras to Lausanne, Switzerland, where we live.

And because of this womb-bond between brothers and sisters, I perceive that in-laws (the strangers, those who come into the family adventitiously) are 'peripheral'. Acceptance of in-laws is dependent upon how much the in-laws are also bonded within the family. And therefore marriage between first cousins, or second cousins, is so prevalent all over India, because it is also part of the family. But now modern times are here; strangers become in-laws. And this gives rise to an intricate status-conferring problem that cannot even be discussed. Can we, the outer comets, the in-laws, really become revolving satellite moons, in harmony with the main, compact planet?

Either in-laws become part of the Family, or they remain, in subtly unspoken ways, outsiders, or 'outlaws'. The nearest I got to knowing that Caro, Vincent's first wife, had not really been 'in' was when Theresa remarked that 'she would never play cards with us'. Cards means rummy. Yet this does not mean being rejected, ostracized, ignored. It does mean that in those subtly unspoken ways which are Indian, when questions of importance arise, the Family sides with its own, and there is total mutism where in-laws are concerned.

18

It was almost impossible for me, faced with such a challenge, not to want to be partly ingested, incorporated, within the Family, and of course, with my Chinese upbringing, I too knew the power of silence, the power of non-words. Of just being, without talking.

The Family. So fleshily, burstingly, uproariously Indian, but also a Catholic family with its own taboos. Never marry on a Tuesday or a Saturday, and not between 4 and 6 p.m. on Sunday. Adapted from Indian traditional good and bad days, nefarious and propitious hours. The Catholics have none of the food inhibitions of Hindus or Muslims, and so the Family ate everything, including beef; for in India there is the killing of cows, but only by Muslims. But this meant that the servants, too, must be Catholic.

Being Dravidians,* or dark South Indians, they shared a cultural heritage of song, dance, literature, music, and handicrafts far preceding the Aryan invasion of India round about 2,000 B.C. The Dravidians claim (and it seems they are right) that the great civilizations of Mohenjo-daro and Harappa were built by them, and that they were mentioned as 'heaven' in the Epic of Gilgamesh, which is considered, in American universities, as the first epic of the white, Aryan races. In this continual, and continued, struggle between the races, which is the Indian caste system, the Dravidians of South India have achieved their own identity.

Tamil, or Dravidian, art and culture have made Madras a centre for the arts. The number of cinemas in Tamil Nadu (the state of the Tamils, Madras being the capital), is twice the national average *per capita*. Tamil Nadu is also reckoned one of the most industrially developed areas in India. There is also a higher average of literacy there than in other parts of India, bar another southern state, Kerala, where literacy is the highest of all.

---

* Dravidians: the original inhabitants of India before the Aryan invasion which occurred 4,000 years ago. They include the Tamils and other South Indian groups.

In this setting, traditional feasts and festivals are shared between all communities, which here, of course, means religions. The Family would celebrate not only Christmas and Easter, but all the several new years (Hindu, Muslim, solar), the Harvest Festival of Ponggol, and many others. It was in Madras that, visiting a local Indian Jesuit who was doing a dissertation on Muslim traders to China, I found him rehearsing a local dance with young seminarists. All of them dancing away to the sound of drums and flute.

I would join the celebrations whenever I was in Madras. But presence at anniversaries, weddings, funerals, does not really mean kinship. It was also apparent to me that kinship extended through the mother, through the mother's family. This would be a throwback to the old *Maruma-kathaia*, or mother-system, the matriarchal society which prevailed in South India for a very long time. Two of Vincent's sisters would marry their first cousins on the mother's side, thus knitting family bonds in the traditional way. This kind of cousinly marriage is exceedingly common in India, but nowhere more so than among the Catholic community, the most conservative of all.

There was one family activity in which I could join; symbolic, time-consuming, but oh, so rewarding in the end. That was playing rummy. Playing rummy together, in groups of six or ten, winning and losing against each other, seems one of the Family's rituals of togetherness. Cards in hand, round a small table, I could feel them, see them, as one does a sea anemone, or one of those magnificent composite sea creatures which are both colonies and yet individuals. I like to play cards, mahjong, bridge, poker. Without any talent for winning. I lose, but I observe. And so I played rummy. How else could I reach them? Become part of them? They would, for so many years, treat me as an honoured guest, give me their eager attention, as if every word I spoke was important. But was I really part of them?

When I landed at an Indian airport, there would be a

sister, two, three; a brother or two, various husbands and wives (in-laws recruited for the purpose), sometimes the children, forming a loose but perfectly visible welcome crowd among the hundreds of expectant welcomers. For in India to see someone off at the airport, or to welcome them in, is still standard procedure, and at times around 200 people will congregate to send off a renowned *sadhu* or politician.

One or two garlands round my neck; one or two brothers wresting a piece of luggage away from me. And then, though none of them are wealthy, the notion of money having passed them by, they would buy presents for me. And ask me to huge meals (they are all excellent trencher-men) which they could scarcely afford. They exuded a feeling of ease, courtesy, elegance. For Appa, not caring about money, had insisted on education for all his children, including the girls, who had all been to university.

Thus the Family. Catholic, but Indian. Practising in some ways what the Brahmins also practised: kinship, intermarriage with the matrilineal line. Keeping to customs and traditions. Dravidian, but with a strong infusing of a religion which, in the end, is universal.

The next generation, however, is turning out differently. The young sons and daughters are beginning to marry out of the religion, out of caste. This chagrins very much the archbishop at the cathedral. For what will happen to *their* children? Will they be Catholics, or something else?

To marry 'across the line' is still quite extraordinary. But Appa does not rebuke.

I have a passion for research. Perhaps because my Chinese family has kept its genealogy book for almost eight centuries. But in India – save for the royal houses – there is little concern for keeping family records, since Death is but return to that Great Pool of Incessant Transformation, exemplified by the dancing god Shiva, who dances the perpetual Dance of Life.

I went hunting for the antecedents of Vincent's family. I

21

found out that Appa's grandfather had a house in Royapuram, a town by the sea, now an important part of the port of Madras. There Catholics driven out from Mylapore by the British had congregated in the eighteenth century. I went to Royapuram, to search for the house.

I found the church. The Church of the Holy Mother of Royapuram, first a chapel, built with funds from the Catholic community, maintained by them for some two centuries. A handsome edifice, with a wavy roof, inspired by the sea waves, and thirty-nine crosses jutting from every possible protuberance. Its windows went from the roof down to the tiled floor, giving great ventilation. The church was really established by the boat-owners; which means those who, through tremendous exertion, had become owners of their own boats, and thus escaped low-caste fisherman status. But, in turn, the Catholics practised the caste system: and untouchables, new converts, still crouched or squatted on the tiles, denied chairs and benches, set apart from the rest of the congregation. The horrendous supremacy of the caste system is not perceptible to Westerners on a visit; it is only perceptible when one truly penetrates (even superficially) Indian society.

Today, the church of Royapuram has been remodelled. Alas. The roof has been modernized, and looks like any ordinary roof. The crosses are gone. It has been painted in grey and white 'for the tourists'. Yet Royapuram remains a quaint oasis of an indeterminate time between two conquests. Along its tree-shaded streets the houses are Portuguese-Indian in style. I find the house of Appa's father, near a chapel, now derelict and used by a printing company to store their paper and machinery ...

Thus my new, Indian Family. For am I not in love with their Eldest Son? And shall I not become, one day, Appa's Eldest Daughter-in-law? And to be daughter-in-law in an Indian family is even more important than to be a daughter. The daughter-in-law brings in dowry, influence; serves the family's interests. These are all important notions, never

22

talked about, but active in everyday life. They have their weight of feeling, their links of emotion, their accepted burden of duty.

I have a Chinese family in China; and so many responsibilities towards them. I will now become part of an Indian family in India. I also, through my sisters, through my daughter, who have married Americans, and whose children are American, have an American family in the U.S.A.

Can anyone be heaped with more blessings, with more joyful burdens, than I am?

III

Michael, Peter, Patricia. Vincent's Cheeldren. By Caro Fernandes, that neat, precise woman whose place I took; but who became my very good friend for some years before her death, at the age of eighty, in 1983.

Michael, Peter, Patricia were only names for me for some years. I would ask myself how they felt about me. Certainly they must detest me; a broken home, heartaches … certainly. But they seemed far away, inaccessible.

I first met Michael and his wife Anne in Patna, a town in North India, where Michael was working. Michael had married Anne without finishing his engineering studies, and Vincent, with Appa's emphasis on 'education', had not been happy about the precipitate wedding. He had not attended the marriage ceremony, held in Madras. But Appa and the Family had been there. Without a family, a wedding is not a wedding – neither in China, nor in India. Michael then took some jobs here and there; Anne had a baby within the first year of their marriage, and then two more, all three of them sons. Anne is small, thin, excessively fine-boned.

She took some years to recover from three labours in rapid succession; her pelvic bones, at the third, gave way, so depleted in calcium had she become. The three boys are handsome and clever; but I am sometimes aware that they regard their grandfather, Vincent, with awe. Yet Vincent does love them, and care for them. However, in a way, he seems disposed to show more affection for his daughter's children (also two sons) than for his son's. It is very hard to explain. I think it is because he feels Michael is his eldest son; and eldest sons are particularly burdened – as he was – with caring for others, and getting less for themselves. This obtains in China too, where eldest sons are supposed to care for the whole family, putting themselves last. But there is also the fact that favouritism happens in all families. All of us are marked by slight differences in parental behaviour towards us. Imperceptible, almost. A tone of voice, a gesture, a certain smile. It all echoes down the corridors of our childhood years. It is often the source of much unfounded bitterness, sibling jealousy.

'I've done as much for Michael, even more, than for my other children,' Vincent says, when I tell him that, too obviously, he dotes upon his daughter. Love is based on a daily confrontation, and it alters daily. But it is also true that there are ways in which parents evaluate their children which are translated as bias, when they are nothing of the kind. Little Lord Fauntleroy was Peter, his mother's favourite. Patricia is lovely, beautiful, and a girl child. And Vincent, being all male, is particularly aware of the need women have for man-caring, for protection. He is a man who wants to protect, to give, to those who need... I needed him, and therefore he came to me.

The need for caring, for being cared for, is something often denied, especially when a woman seems 'independent', and self-reliant, and resourceful. But fundamentally the need remains. Patricia, his daughter, needed her father. It would take me some time to understand why.

Patricia came to Europe on a holiday and stayed with us for some weeks in Paris. Vincent took her out, while I stayed home to type, for I was 'in a book'. Patricia is an extraordinarily beautiful girl; a sepia Sophia Loren, with enormous brown eyes; a loveliness and sweetness about her which is all-Indian, yet with a delicacy of bone which reminds one of the statues found in some temples – not the fulsomely curved ones, but those of young gazelle-like creatures in postures of dance or worship. I realized that she had almost pure Dravidian, or South Indian, features, and her skin, like Vincent's, was dark ... in fact, of that darkness with tinges of blue which I found so entrancing, but which, to my great astonishment, some find repulsive. Especially in India, where the colour complex is stronger, far stronger than in the West; where a dull-featured girl, but with light skin, is still preferred to a darker beauty. Even if, for a while during her presence with us, I was relegated to my type-writer, and occasionally to the kitchen, I had time enough to wonder why Vincent seemed so concerned, so protec-tive, towards his daughter.

Because she was dark. Among the Dravidians of the south there is a rankling feeling that the 'Aryans', the white-skinned invaders of the north, still look down upon them. And they are not far wrong, for in February 1986, in the *New York Times*, the eminent Indian writer Ved Mehta was to tell, in an interview, how he objected to being called 'black', and had retorted that he was an Aryan, descendant of 'white' men ...

To me, Patricia was beautiful; and skin colour only enhanced her loveliness. But Vincent was an Indian father; he feared that she would have less chance of a good match. It took me some time – and a couple of stormy scenes, for I believe in externalizing my feelings – to wrest out of Vincent the reason for his anxious protectiveness. It took a little ingenious bullying to get a coherent explanation.

'You are colour-blind,' said Vincent. 'You don't *see* colour. You only see human beings. But in India, it is not so. I've got to make sure that Patricia studies well; that she has a career ... this will make it easier for her to provide for herself, and to choose a husband.'

So he was walking and talking with his daughter, persuading her of the need to get the best education, to go to university and to become a doctor. 'Then you'll always be able to look after yourself, in case ... '

This strange Indian hang-up on colour I would understand better when, one day, an Indian friend said to me reproachfully (he was, of course, an 'Aryan', or thought he was; to me, he was merely olive-brownish): 'Han Suyin, of course we're so pleased you chose an Indian, but why such a *dark* Indian?'

I had replied: 'Is he really dark? I've never been aware of that.'

And on another occasion a 'fair-complexioned' Indian woman said to me, in an *enjoué* tone of forced lightness: 'I would not want a man who leaves a dark rim round the tub after a bath.'

So at last I understood Vincent's concern for his daughter ... but it took me time, and I was, for a while, resentful. Jealousy, suspicion, is something unavoidable except in very extraordinary people. And I am only too human.

And then there was Peter.

Since, after all, it is Peter I am concerned with in this book, the way in which he came into my life needs to be described. For it was I who was instrumental in getting Peter to go abroad, and hence in shaping his life. And now, very occasionally, Peter, who knows how to hurt, says: 'If I had not left India, I would not have become sick as I am.'

In the spring of 1962 Vincent and I, who were then living in Malaya, drove to Kuala Lumpur, the capital, to visit the British High Commissioner in Malaya and his wife, Sir Anthony and Viscountess Dorothea Head. Dorothea had written to me, written that she wanted to paint my portrait. We had met at a party where she and I had both been very bored. She wanted to see me again.

Kuala Lumpur was a growing, thriving place. Tall buildings were replacing the charming wooden houses raised on stilts above ground; the forest and swamps beyond Muddy Mouth (the meaning of Kuala Lumpur) were disappearing as shops sprouted along the new roads, and behind them new settlements. Independence had come to Malaya in 1957, and I had great regard and personal affection for the Prime Minister, Tunku (Prince) Abdul Rahman. His Australian secretary, Frank Sullivan, was a collector of Malayan art and now, with independence, came cultural assertion: there were Malay painters and sculptors, and Malay writers. A museum was being established in Kuala Lumpur. I had made donations of some pieces of Ming export Chinese plate to the museum; I bought paintings, on Frank's advice, some merely to encourage the young and eager artists. I had also established a scholarship for a Chinese student to learn Malay at Nanyang University in Singapore. Nanyang University, entirely funded by the Overseas Chinese of Singapore and Malaya, had been established to challenge the 'English only' colonial trend in the University of Singapore. But I felt that harmony between the races could only be achieved if Nanyang University also had courses in Malay for the Chinese students. Likewise, Tunku Abdul Rahman had kindly accepted from me another scholarship for a Malay to learn Chinese, in order to promote racial harmony ...

Going to Kuala Lumpur, therefore, was always pleasant for me. Dorothea Head was a true-blue English aristocrat, which means that she commented on everything in a loud voice, and never cared who heard. She greeted us when we arrived, dressed in a loose robe, her hands paint-smudged, surrounded by dogs, cats and some wonderful African birds with aigrettes upon their heads. 'My dear, I've really wanted to meet you to talk about China. I know you go there, although it's quite, quite taboo and lots of people think you're a communist, but I know you're not. But do tell me, because I want to go, although Anthony won't let me.'

Anthony Head came walking towards us in a dressing-gown. He had been in the swimming pool and a parrot was perched upon his shoulder. He offered a dip in the pool. I declined, saying I did not like pools. 'People sometimes pee in the water.'

'Aha, but there's a powder you can put in. The water turns yellow round the culprit,' he retorted.

Dorothea did paint my picture. Later she would go to China, as soon as Anthony had retired from the diplomatic service. I still have her portrait of me in my possession, as I also have one that Hussein, the Indian painter, did of me.

We went to see the Heads quite often, every time I went to Kuala Lumpur to call upon Tunku Abdul Rahman, who was always very kind to me. We were also at one, thinking that the Prime Minister of Singapore, Lee Kuan Yew, was a bit too pushy. 'He always wants to win, even at golf,' Tunku chuckled. Lee Kuan Yew was exerting himself at the time to try to merge Singapore and Malaya. It was a complex situation, and since at the same time Lee expressed some contempt for the Malays, it seemed to me highly dubious that there would be a merger; especially since, had this been realized, there would have been more people of Chinese racial origin, in Malaya-Singapore, than Malays ... I knew the Malays were very much against it, and I said so. Which earned me, I think, the ire of Lee Kuan Yew and subsequently led to our departure from the area.

As we sat one day, Dorothea, Anthony, Vincent and I, the subject of Vincent's son Peter cropped up. Vincent knew that Peter was brilliant; and he felt that it would be a good thing for Peter to go to England to take a higher degree. Forthwith Anthony offered to sponsor him, and wrote a letter recommending Peter.

And thus it happened that, in 1966, Peter went to Rugby, to do his Ph.D. in engineering. And that is how Destiny, Karma, used me, my connection with the Heads,

29

in fashioning subsequent events in Peter's life.

As I have explained, Vincent had finally obtained a good position as engineer with Jardine Waugh in Singapore. He drove every day from our house in Johor Bahru, across the Causeway which links Singapore to Malaya, and back. These were days of ease, and all went well. In September-October 1962 I was invited to Japan for a two-week tour by the Japanese Ministry for External Affairs. And it was during those two weeks that border fighting broke out between India and China.

Vincent telephoned me in Tokyo from Malaya. He might be recalled to India, he said. After all, he had been a colonel in the Indian army, as well as an engineer, and was still on the reserve list although he had retired in 1959. I returned to Malaya to find that the Chinese, with consummate sense of timing, after having repulsed the Indian armies which had been told by Nehru to advance, had themselves deliberately withdrawn behind the line purporting to represent the 'frontier' in dispute, and were now calling for negotiations.

But at the time no one would say a good word for 'Red' China. Although it would become very clear that there had been no Chinese 'invasion', this was how things were represented by almost all the world media. The U.S.S.R., which was on bad terms with China, and cultivating India, also did not help. Consequently, on my return from Japan, I found the Overseas Chinese community in Singapore, and especially the students of Nanyang University, confused and upset by the bias in the reporting. Had China really treacherously attacked an unprepared India? Sedulously, the Singapore press gave this version of events ... a version now known to be incorrect.

In that December and January I was asked by Nanyang University professors to explain what had really happened. By then, I had fully documented both versions. I had taken the trouble to read both the Indian newspapers, which reported Prime Minister Nehru ordering the Indian army to advance *ten days* before the supposed Chinese invasion, and the Chinese press (banned in Singapore and Malaya – anyone with a Chinese newspaper in their possession went to jail for two years – but somehow obtainable from England).

Vincent was asked to state his views as an Indian, and all he said was: 'India and China are two very old countries with a long history of friendship. There have been some border incidents which, I am sure, will be settled in the future.' He was, in fact, quoting Prime Minister Nehru himself, who had said something like that in the Lok Sabha (the lower house of the Indian parliament, equivalent to the House of Commons), some months previously.

And this innocuous phrase would lead to much trouble. For it was clear that 'someone' wanted an opportunity to do me harm. In May 1963 Jardine Waugh renewed Vincent's contract, and at the same time gave him four weeks' holiday which, of course, Vincent used to go to India to see his family while I remained to run my medical clinic and also to finish a book. On his return in June, however, he was prevented from landing in Singapore. 'Someone' had banned him, he was accused of having 'said things disturbing to racial harmony'. But nothing could ever be obtained in writing. It was all airy words, from one or two officials I saw ... later we realized that 'someone' had also accused Vincent of 'treason' towards his own country, India. Fortunately his own government, whose intelligence services in Malaya were well-informed, ignored the accusation. Despite the fact that anti-Chinese hysteria prevailed in some areas of India (notably in Calcutta, where 14,000 Chinese shopkeepers and restaurant owners had a rather hard time), no measures were taken against Vincent.

In Malaya Tunku Abdul Rahman most generously allowed Vincent's return. But we both realized the squeeze would continue. Vincent, meanwhile, had of course lost his job since he could not cross the Causeway to go to

Singapore. Hence we moved. To Hong Kong in 1964. I wound up my clinic, abandoning medicine after fourteen years of practice, and not without sorrow. We were to remain in Hong Kong for some three years, before I decided that the best place for me would be Switzerland, where I could really work without hindrance, and at the same time keep in touch with the whole world.

This was the beginning of a fruitful dislocation; more than ever, I would be able to roam the planet, to travel, and now with Vincent. China, India, South-East Asia, Europe ... and now America beckoned. Almost coincidental with our departure from Malaya came an invitation for me to lecture in the United States. To attend seminars on China at prestigious universities in the U.S.A. The Vietnam war was, I think, focusing attention on Asia; the role of China was being hotly debated; and there was, as I would find out, also a great deal of debate as to the outcome of the Vietnam war.

Had I remained in Malaya, I think I might not have become so flexible, so able to move and so free in my movements. We spent, Vincent and I, some happy three years, in which I did a great deal of lecturing as well as writing some books, while based in Hong Kong. We then removed to Europe; where Lausanne, in Switzerland, became my base, but this meant that it was possible for us to spend weeks, even months, in Paris and London, and of course also in the U.S.A.

And that is how in August of 1967, Peter, who had spent some time studying in England, landed in Paris. And he landed precisely when his father had left for India for Appa's birthday. Appa's birthday was on August 15 and Vincent would try never to miss it. I occasionally missed it, of course. And that year of 1967 I did not feel like rejoicing in India, for the Cultural Revolution in China, begun the previous year, was now reaching a climax, and I had just been refused a visa to return to China ...

I was therefore feeling rather miserable, but also pressurized to finish a book, when Peter landed in Paris.

August in Paris is splendid. Many Parisians are away; those who remain are free of that usual snappiness, a gritty behaviour which begins to afflict this hard-working and highly vital people round June, when foreigners flood the city and the Parisians are longing for their *vacances*. Paris in August is mild, good-tempered, with soft streets, and chestnut trees moving thick foliage in the evening breeze. Great droves of tourists do not seem to crowd Paris, and though restaurants are closed, the boulevards are beautiful at night and the floodlit beauty of Notre-Dame, of the Panthéon, of the Eiffel Tower, really make one happy to be alive.

Peter came in saying, 'Hello.' A good-looking, tall young man. Not as Dravidian-looking as his father. He could easily have been a Spaniard, a Portuguese, a Levantine. His skin was much lighter than Vincent's, possibly due to his mother, Caro, who certainly had some Portuguese and possibly even English ancestry. After being shown his room and the bathroom, he unpacked and settled into a stolid mutism which I would now have to break.

Why had he come? Because he was on holiday. He would remain till his father returned. Yes, he was fit. He strolled among my books, discovered a French–English dictionary, and plunged himself into it.

Cocooning silence. At first it did not bother me. The younger generation in India learn to be silent when their elders are about. Peter replied monosyllabically to my enquiries about his journey, whether he had clothes to wash (no), and what he would like for dinner (anything). I felt, however, that he was trying hard *not* to speak to me. Perhaps shyness. We were strangers. Perhaps he was watching me. After another day, when he would still answer exactly, politely, but without a word more than necessary the usual questions as to whether he had slept well (yes, thank you), whether he wanted coffee or tea, whether he had perused the *Guide de Paris* I had thrust in his hands, I

33

decided that he was waiting for me to do something. He wanted me to make the first move, to break the walls of non-words he was erecting round him.

'Why don't you speak up, Peter?'

He looked surprised. 'I don't know what to say.'

'That's true. You don't know what to say. Because you might say something silly – is that why?'

'No, it's …' He glanced at me, then away, measuring every word. 'I find it strange to be here. In Paris.'

I took him for walks, walks in the delightful Paris of August. I talked. I became a glib, eloquent tourist guide. We went to the Louvre and the Tuileries; I made him look at paintings, sculptures. We went up and down the Champs-Élysées. We went to bookshops and bought paperbacks. We went to small restaurants, and I made him eat snails. He said: 'I've never eaten snails.'

'Well now you have.'

In between jaunts I worked on my book, and since my cleaning woman was on holiday, Peter and I cleaned the apartment. This he did with unbelievable meticulousness. I put him to dusting my books, and he did them one by one … it took him the best part of three days. Now he went out alone, in the afternoons. He contrived to be so noiseless when he was sitting in his own room that it unnerved me. He would close doors quietly; I could not hear the handle turn, the tongue slide into its catch. He was a presence trying to be unpresent, but trying too hard. And all the time, I felt, there was something he wanted to tell me.

I had an advantage – his father's absence. Hence a lack of Authority with a big A. On my trips to India with Vincent the pattern of authority was always there. Vincent's sisters and brothers sought his advice, seldom (never) contradicted him. Their husbands, or wives, would also appear to defer to Vincent. As for the young ones, they never talked back at all. The only person who openly, persistently, challenged and contradicted and bullied Vincent was me.

'Don't you ever argue with Vincent?' I had asked one day

34

in Madras while the odours of curry wafted us hungrily to the table, and the last rummy hand of the night was being played.

Vincent had turned his dazzling, amused, loving, infuriating smile upon me, proudly, and said something in Tamil which probably meant: 'See, see, look at her, she has to argue everything ... ' He was pleased that I should thus demonstrate my spirit, being the only one allowed to do so, to go against him. The smile meant, of course, that no one else in the family would be so silly. 'Look what an entertaining person I've brought to you,' the smile seemed to say. Everyone looked at me with benign affection and then talked of something else ...

I did not want Peter to bring this attitude with him to my house, to defer to me, keeping his thoughts to himself.

Peter's silence was, I thought, part of the 'Yes, Daddy' routine by which Michael and he agreed with their father. 'Yes' ... 'Yes' ... Now Peter said 'Yes' to me, merely in acknowledgment that he heard my voice. We dawdled along the Seine; I asked him, had he seen the Thames? 'Yes.' We went in and out of Notre-Dame. We shopped, cooked, and on the fifth day I felt I had given him enough time.

It was after an excellent lunch (again snails for hors-d'oeuvre) that I broke through. 'I guess it's difficult for you, Peter, talking to me. You probably resent me, because I took your mother's place.'

He looked at the snail shells; he had disposed them meticulously all round his plate. He nodded slowly. His whole body changed, became less stiff. He seemed to straighten up.

'Yes, I hated you. When I was growing up. Because of Mummy.'

So much later, eighteen years later, in 1985, in that clarity and ruthlessness of unfettered emotion which illness has brought upon him, he would at last tell me: 'You know, you know, when people heard that Daddy and Mummy were divorcing, they treated us like lepers ... ' and then:

35

'Why did you have to come and hurt us so much?'

But in that Paris, I was already trying to exorcize the spectres of hatred and I said to Peter: 'But you don't hate me now. You don't hate me, and it bothers you that you cannot hate me.'

He did not reply, but seemed once again to curl in upon himself. Like a snail re-entering its shell.

'I'm sorry for your mother. It's not her fault. It's mine. We've all got to learn never to justify ourselves. Not in the name of love or in any other name. I'm not justifying myself. I accept that I also do evil. But you're here, and you've come because you wanted to see what I was like, and now you're angry with yourself because you don't hate me as you should.'

He concentrated upon the snail shells. The next morning he appeared with a small bunch of violets held tight in his grip. 'For you.'

Perhaps Peter would learn to accommodate the complexity of his feelings towards me. But it would not be easy. He was intense, honest; possessed of a meticulous integrity which required perfection in all things he did. He found it difficult to have to be less than perfect in all that he did and thought. He found it very difficult to have to hate, and to love, at the same time, the same person.

'Don't hate your father, Peter.'

'Daddy's always had his way,' says Peter.

'Because none of you argue with him.'

He looked away.

We played Scrabble. He took ten minutes, fifteen minutes, to make a move. Pondering, searching, calculating, hesitating. Not impulsive or impatient. Afraid of being beaten. As I watched him, I became a little apprehensive. With this kind of mind, how would Peter ever cope with the multitudinous betrayals, large and small, which are the very fabric of living? And also of loving? For love does not dwell but in a realm of half-lies. Eager, beloved lies ...

'It's only a game, Peter; come on.'

36

But not for Peter. He cut his steak in small, equal slices before eating it. Reduction of all things to finite blocks. The curls, Little Lord Fauntleroy, being expected to have high marks. To be faultless. Peter. Who could do no wrong.

He was worried by religion. He had wanted to be a priest, his father had told me. 'Nothing doing, you'll be an engineer,' Daddy had said.

'Yes, Daddy.'

Now Peter said: 'I wanted to be a priest, Suyin. But I wasn't good enough.'

'Have you any girl friends, Peter?' We were walking to a midnight film in one of those small French cinemas; there was always room in a cinema house in August.

'Why do you ask?' He turned, a half-smile upon his face. He now took long strides, away from me.

'Well, it's only natural ... '

Abruptly he put his hands in his pockets. 'I can't talk about it.'

'Okay, don't. I was just asking.' And then, perversely, gaily, I talked about my lovers and husbands before his father. 'Believe me, Peter, some are lucky and first love is last love, and others are for ever growing and coming to the end of a person, of a love.'

Now we could even have something like a dialogue, if a dialogue can be constructed on an abundance of words, on the one side, and the least possible amount, on the other.

Peter would say: 'Family planning with mechanical means is a mortal sin.'

'I think it's truly deadly to load a woman with unwanted children, Peter.'

He would ponder over this. For days. Two months later, on another visit, he told me he was in favour of family planning: 'But only by self-control I think it can be done.'

'I think you're asking far too much of human beings.'

He thought, and smiled: 'I think everyone in our family has practised family planning,' he chuckled. But would not elaborate.

37

Patricia came again, on yet another visit, beautiful as ever, and now beginning to study medicine. She was also a good hockey player, and full of joy. She went to Italy with Vincent and some friends. And once again, I became somewhat irate.

'Vincent, you're ruining your daughter's emotional life ... you've got to detach her from you.'

But I was too Freudian in my appraisal. The resilience, the flexibility of the large Family also understands, encompasses, in its womb opacity, all these phenomena. I made it very clear to Patricia, when she returned, that unless she broke away a little from 'Daddy' she would not achieve adulthood.

'You are right,' Patricia said. 'I can't go on clinging to Daddy. I know it.' Wonderful Patricia. Clear-headed, self-aware. She thus earned my respect and affection: she had the courage and intelligence to face up to a situation, and her response was very swift. With Peter I would always have to wait, a very long time.

I had no compunction about stating aloud, once or twice in Madras, that the Indian Big Family is fundamentally 'incestuous'. All families are, to one degree or another, but Big Families are a world of emotional links within themselves, they are wrought and intertwined to a degree which no Indian writer has yet dared to explore to the full. Where the bonds between brother and sister are so strong, so are the links between father and daughter, son and mother. In fact, I was told (and it was a true story) of an Indian mother who kept her son in her bed till his wedding day. And on the night after the wedding, having consulted the soothsayers and found the hours of darkness unpropitious, she made her son sleep by her side, while the new bride slept on a pallet on the bedroom floor.

And my friend Saraswathi, who is a Brahmin, has also told me how a mother, and her sisters, pass the male children they have from hand to hand, to fondle them, especially their genitalia. For the cult of the lingam, the penis, makes such caresses prayer, adoration.

'Incestuous,' I had said aloud. 'Emotionally so, of course, not in actual practice, but you've got to know it.'

And the Family had stared, and nodded their heads from side to side, not a bit incensed or shocked.

'That's right.' Basil, Vincent's brother, had grinned. He and I also got on well. 'It's quite true.'

Patricia had been on 'Daddy's' side in the matter of the divorce. Nothing Daddy did was ever wrong. It was I who reconciled her to her mother.

'There is no right or wrong, Patricia. There is only a situation.' And when Patricia asked me to her wedding, in 1975, I made sure that her own mother, too, was there, and in the reception line.

Thus, by fits and starts, in segments, I came to know the cheeldren. In between writing books, travels with Vincent, lectures, trips to China, I made time to drop in upon the Family, and to see the cheeldren.

Peter and I got on very well; perhaps because he too, like his grandfather, Appa, was concerned with social issues, as I was. Perhaps because, like myself, he was obsessed with work well done. But Appa had immense tolerance, and an eclectic approach to life. I had much experience of how the best theories go awry and good intentions produce evil results. I never expected too much of others. But Peter was aspiring to perfection without ambiguity, without compromise. Flaws in those he loved distressed him, although an innate sweetness, a disposition for affection, would come to temper him. I think that in some way he felt guilty for other people's misdeeds. I hope not for mine. I have a faint suspicion (and perhaps in another few years he will tell me whether my suspicion is correct) that Peter has been praying to God for my soul to be saved, and possibly, possibly, offered himself in sacrifice, to redeem all sinners ... but I do not know.

IV

Writing about Peter is also writing about myself. For authors, when describing someone, are delineating their own reactions to the character under scrutiny. Peter's destiny is intertwined with mine; for I have intervened, have been a causal factor, in shaping his future. Karma. And now, once again, it was through me that he subsequently remained in Europe to work as an engineer for some years.

My friend Frederic Dahlmann, whom I had known since 1954, came to dinner with us in 1967. Dahlmann's father, a German, was a 'China trader', and had bundled off his young son Frederic to Shanghai in 1935. Hitler had come to power in Germany, and Dahlmann father was greatly worried, for young Freddi was a member of a German leftist party – a fashion for many young men of good family in the 1930s, whether in England or in Germany.

Jews and communists were being hunted down in Germany. The Dahlmanns appear to have shifted their fortune in good time, much of it to Sweden, some of it to Shanghai. Young Freddi would remain in Shanghai for many years;

until 1951, two years after the communist armies of Mao Zedong came to power.

Freddi Dahlmann had not given up his idealistic notion of a world of total equality; though he would combine this with the most astute and successful capitalist practices in business. Like Armand Hammer, and other 'Red capitalists', he both helped the new-risen worlds of Soviet Russia and China, and at the same time procured extremely good contracts for Western businessmen. He was involved, while in Shanghai, in helping some of the hunted-down communists and saving their lives, during the military dictatorship of Chiang Kai-shek. But when in 1949 the Communist People's Liberation Army marched into Shanghai, he was arrested. 'They did not know who I was, or what I had done,' says Freddi, still chortling as he remembers those days when, manacled, he was flung in jail and ordered to confess his crimes. But he was released when some upper members of the Party recognized him as a bona fide businessman, who had indeed helped some of them to escape death. During the Korean war, Freddi Dahlmann, like some other European and Hong Kong businessmen, had quietly conveyed some useful goods, such as penicillin, to China, despite the total American embargo, which made even goods for humanitarian purposes prohibited from being imported into China.

Freddi had a good many sons and daughters from several marriages. His family was a fascinating *mélange* of nations: German, Belgian, Swiss, Swedish, and even African. Many a poor country has found that Freddi Dahlmann and his sons (for they too are involved in the dynasty of business founded by their grandfather) devise beneficial industrial schemes, and are useful at arranging loans on better credit terms for projects.

Freddi Dahlmann and his sons are forever travelling. I would meet Freddi in Hong Kong, Paris, London, or Beijing, Singapore, or Brussels. China was a bond between us, since he had been there so many years. His houses were

41

full of precious antiques. He was – like Armand Hammer – a discerning collector. His conversation was entrancing, with anecdotes of every country where he had swung deals, bought or sold anything from telephones to tar, and met almost everyone from presidents to Red Guards. We ran into each other in Paris and it seemed only natural that, at a pleasant dinner at the Grand Vefour, Freddi would say to Vincent: 'Send us your son, Vincent. We need competent engineers from Asia. We want to train them, so that they can help us in our expansion. We would find Peter useful, and he would have a good future with us.' Freddi was much aware of the need for technical personnel in China, in India and in Africa; where one day Western businesses would have to look for growing markets. Vincent also felt that this would benefit Peter. In India, he would be well regarded and also very useful to any Indian company, should he have had some experience abroad. And Indian engineers were more acceptable in Zaire, in Libya, in Iran, and in other places, than Western personnel.

Freddi thus offered Peter a training job, first with A.C.E.C., a Belgian engineering company sited in Charleroi, with links to American and other companies. A.C.E.C. was engaged in many projects overseas, some in areas where European engineers did not do so well because of cultural differences. There were sensitive areas in the world where the wives of technical personnel found it very hard to live; Peter was, so far, unmarried.

At the end of 1968 Peter therefore went to Belgium, and trained there till 1970. He came to see me several times, dropping into my apartment in Lausanne, where I had become resident in 1969. Always he brought presents: a pure gold Dunhill lighter. An Hermès scarf. A Moroccan bag, the leather fine as silk. We talked. Of politics and people, of China and India, of the Vietnam war, of music … when I say we talked, I mean that he asked questions, which involved my trying to explain things. He was, in many ways, quite naive, unwilling to accept that in the

42

world the affairs of men were never straightforward; that politics was a tortuous business. His word output was always scanty, but perhaps now he talked more than he had ever before done to someone older than himself. He also spoke more readily with his father of technical matters, of his friends in Belgium. He seemed to be unwinding, but he never talked much about himself. He was always tremendously helpful, wanting to do jobs for me, and he never queried my work. The act of writing seemed to him something I did, which needed no comment on his part, and no query. His lack of curiosity about certain things, such as the creative process, or psychological motivation, was probably because he had channelled himself so much into engineering, and mathematics. But he was observant, however wrong the conclusion of his observations. Fifteen years later, in 1985, he would burst out one day as I took him out for his evening walk:

'You know, when I came to stay with you ... I saw you and Daddy argue, fight ... I'd never thought married people would argue so much with each other ... I was sure it wouldn't last between you ... at most two, three years.' He shook his head in wonderment, still convinced that people did not behave in that way in a real marriage.

'It's the couples who never argue, never fight, who stow it all away inside, who don't last,' I said.

And he laughed then, throwing his head back, still full of surprise, and went pacing ahead, struggling to put down his old ghosts, to reconcile the set image he had of what a man–woman relationship should be, to the relationship he saw between his father and myself.

I also had a small apartment in the Swiss mountains, in a place called Flims, a beautiful small village in the Grisons mountains, one of the most pleasant ski resorts of Switzerland. Freddi Dahlmann owned two large chalets in Flims, his sister had two apartments there, so that it seemed natural for me also to have a place there. At Christmas, in the summer, the Dahlmanns would congregate in Flims; there would be birthdays and other celebrations, and I could also work easily in the quiet of the snow-clad circus of mountains which surrounded the village. The silence was so profound, especially off-season, when one would meet no one on the mountain pathways, that one's ears became singularly acute. I could hear a thrush shake its wings, and the stir of a squirrel scampering among the pine trees.

Those years of 1968 to 1970 were productive, but also years of hidden anxiety for me. The Cultural Revolution was proceeding; Freddi Dahlmann had been to China, but I had been refused a visa in 1967 and 1968, and the rumour was spread that I was an 'American agent'.

In 1968 the American writer, Edgar Snow (he, too, was not allowed to go to China, despite having written that excellent book *Red Star Over China* which popularized the epic history of Mao Zedong's leadership of the Red Armies, and the famous Long March) and myself were invited to lecture in the U.S.A., and it then became evident that there was a change in foreign policy thinking in Washington. The Vietnam war was dragging on, but many were now disenchanted with it in the United States. On the west coast, some businessmen were grumbling that all the business in China would go to Europe; Europe itself was restive with American restrictions on selling goods to communist countries, especially since in 1964 General de Gaulle had officially recognized the Peoples Republic of China.

In 1969 I was again invited, by the Chinese ambassador in Paris, to go to China. 'Things are getting better,' he said, ambiguously. Vincent could not go; Indian passports, because of the frontier conflict of 1962, were made invalid by the Indian government for going to China. I went, therefore, and spent almost three months there; and I was asked, when I returned to Europe, to convey a message to General de Gaulle, inviting him to go to Beijing. Unfortunately, the French Ministry of Foreign Affairs did not seem to take the message seriously; I appealed, finally, to a great personal friend of de Gaulle, the economist

44

Jacques Rueff. Time passed; when de Gaulle finally got the message, he was ill, and died soon afterwards.

Peter came and went, always delightful to have around; something like the son I had never had. I teased him and went for walks with him; and he looked happy. It was during an interlude when Peter was with us that a letter, addressed to me, from Belgium, came to the house. It was written by a girl, Y., who stated in the letter that she wanted to marry Peter. She loved him. She appealed to me to help her.

'Nonsense,' said Vincent crisply. 'Don't answer the letter. It's Peter's business, anyway.'

'But the girl sounds desperate.' I confronted Peter. 'Who is she, Peter? Did you sleep with her? Do you want to marry her?'

'I slept with her but I don't want to marry her.'

I said: 'Well, I'm glad you made up your mind at last to have a girl friend.'

He looked away, his face obstinate. He had done something wrong. It was a sin, by his upbringing, by his religious code, to sleep with someone outside marriage. It was a failure, a flaw; he would do his best to erase this flaw. Which was to refuse to acknowledge it.

'I don't want to marry her.'

'If you don't want to, there's nothing much I can say, can I? Anyway I guess you were not her first boy friend, were you?'

I was away on a two-day jaunt when the girl came to the apartment house and stood at the door, waiting for me. For some hours. The concierge told me when I returned. Concierges love gossip. Her eyes sparkled with ill-satisfied curiosity. 'A woman waited for you. I told her you were not in.' What else was said between them I shall never know.

Peter must have talked. Talked of me to the girl. Given my name, my address. He had talked of me to her. Why? Otherwise, how would she have found me? And why did

45

he talk about me? And what did he say to her about me?

'I don't want to marry her,' repeated Peter. His face set, an unyielding geometry of bone and muscle under the olive skin. Complete non-cooperation. No way to budge him. Oh Peter.

Despite Vincent's opposition, I did write to the girl, because it seemed to me that as a woman I ought to help another woman. I told her that Peter seemed decided not to marry her, that it was something I could not force him to do, and that I was very sorry. I gave the letter to Vincent to post. Did it ever reach her? Or did he decide that it would be in Peter's best interests for me not to reply? I had to leave it to him. Head of the Clan. Father.

'When you go back to Belgium, try to work out something,' I said to Peter.

Peter's training at A.C.E.C. had not been without some hitches. Some of them were due to the Belgian staff, who had put him to work as an inferior grade engineer, when his Indian degrees, recognized in England, qualified him for other tasks. Peter, however, refused to complain or to protest. This was surprising to me. 'Why don't you do something about this, Peter? You don't like it, you tell your father about it, but you cannot expect your father to talk to the company for you.'

'I don't want to fight. They're my friends,' Peter replied. And this was the way it was. Though something was slightly unfair, he would not protest.

'You don't relish battling.'

'There is no happiness in fighting.'

'There is, there is ... you simply have not tried. You've had it quite easy all your life, Peter. School, college, university, then jobs. Just try to fight like me, fight your way out ...'

He laughed. 'You like fighting, you even fight my daddy,' he said.

'Your daddy would be bored with a woman who'd never talk back at him ... someone like an Indian cow.'

46

His skin darkened, which meant he was flushing. I noticed his lashes were not as long as his father's.

'Why, why an Indian cow?'

'They're so placid. All cows are. I don't ask you to walk over other people, but to stand up for yourself. You say you want to do something for the poor, for the exploited. Well, it must all begin with an assertion of your own self, of what you are.'

It seemed to me that the distinction between knowing one's own worth and fighting for it, and aggressiveness towards others, which meant the suppression of the helpless, the subordinate, the weak, especially in a caste-ridden society such as India's, was blurred in Peter's mind. He was so full of social conscience, but even he, at times (and especially later, when he became ill), would assume towards servants that peremptory tone which seems so normal in India, which I find all the time among my many Indian friends, and of which they are themselves unaware. It is a change of register; it is almost impalpable; it also existed in Victorian England, of course.

The girl episode worried me a little. Not too much, but I did not know how Peter would handle it. 'Forget it,' said Vincent. 'Peter does not wish to marry her and there is nothing she can do about it. He's got plenty of girl friends in Bangalore.'

I reminded him that, in India, one did not sleep with 'girl friends'. 'Peter's not slept with a woman before, most probably.'

In 1970 Peter decided to return to India and, regretfully, Freddi let him go. But Y. was persistent. She went to India, turned up in Bangalore. Peter was back at the house, with his sister Patricia, who was studying medicine in Bangalore. The girl was made welcome, and stayed some weeks, enjoying Indian hospitality. She had all her meals, her own room, and no one ever asked her for money or asked her to leave. But Peter totally ignored her. He simply denied her existence.

The outcome was unexpectedly happy. Y. met someone else, fell in love, and married him. And now, at times, when we walk together, Peter and I, he refers to all this:

'She wanted it. She came and took off her clothes and laid down on my bed. I may have a child... maybe I am a father...'

'Well, Peter, you didn't want to marry her, and that's that. She's happy with someone else.'

'Peter will move when the time comes,' said his father, confidently, when his son in 1970, instead of going abroad, elected to return to India. 'He'll marry when he's made up his mind to do so.'

'If he takes as long to make up his mind to marry as he does to play Scrabble, all his girl friends will have given up and found other boys.'

But unlike other Indian fathers, Vincent would not push his children into marriage. He would not hurry Patricia; he insisted that she finish her studies before getting married. 'Then if anything happens, she has a career to fall back on. Because it's terrible for a woman who is a widow and has no training.' In the same way, Vincent would not hurry Peter. Perhaps because in his own generation all marriages were arranged, restricted to a certain community, a certain religion, he would leave his own children free to choose.

The younger generation of the Family are indeed choosing. Despite outward docility, they have contracted love marriages, outside their own religion, which in India is still considered extremely daring, and often leads to family splits. Outside their own caste, outside their own religion, these marriages are called 'mixed marriages', as, in the past, marriages between Westerners and Asians were called. In the staid, profoundly conservative societies that India retains, these are still the exception. And now the children of such 'mixed marriages', and indeed many of the children of Catholic families, are no longer given Western names. Thus, in the Family, the third generation (Vincent's grandchildren) all have Indian names: Romesh and Sunil,

Prathap, Nalin and Vivek... all these are symptomatic of change; although it does not mean that castes are breaking up, or that the social patterns in which Indians move will be profoundly altered.

An Indian engineer, having been abroad and there earned money, is an excellent catch in India. Such a person is automatically destined to get into various enterprises run by private companies, such as Tata, Godrej... When he had returned to India, Peter had been offered a job at an important salary at Tata's.

The Tatas are Parsis, descendants of a priestly Persian family of the Zoroastrian faith. Their business acumen mixes uncommonly well with their strong religious faith, which they keep up. The Parsis form yet another minority, another religious community in multitudinously diverse India, diminutive in number (scarcely 150,000), but powerful due to their enormous economic ability. Nasarwanji Tata, in the early 1850s, set up in business with a Hindu banker-merchant in Bombay. He sent his son, Jamestji, to Elphinstone College, in Scotland. Jamestji, though Anglicized, to the end of his life never abandoned his creed or his black cap and long coat. The crash of 1865 in the cotton boom ruined Nasarwanji, and it took his son seventeen years to repay his father's debts. Jamestji became a contractor for the British army. He had toured the Lancashire cotton mills; and now started India's first cotton spinning and weaving mill. 'What they can do we can also do.' He proceeded to build up with modern machinery, imported from England, the textile industry of Bombay.

From father to son, within the tight, strong web of family, the ruthless determination to build the Tata empire grew. Ventures... into shipping (which failed, for the powerful monopoly of British lines broke Jamestji); into real estate, foreseeing the growth of Bombay into what it is, one of the world's largest and most important cities of international commerce... Tata steel, Tata electric power.

49

The creation of the Indian Institute of Science in Bangalore, with the aim of giving India postgraduate education in science second to none in the world, is due to Tata. Tata today is an intercontinental, far-flung empire. Thus, from generation to generation, Tata linked itself with the future of India, a future in which India would become an industrial power on its own.

Tata offered Peter a good job, at 3,000 rupees a month. A marvellous salary for an Indian engineer. He turned it down.

Instead, Peter stayed in Bangalore, and joined the Myrada, the Mysore State Resettlement and Agricultural Agency. In 1970 there was much talk of promoting agriculture: India's 'green revolution' was about to begin. For three years, till 1973, Peter would work at Myrada. It was at that time that he would read a great deal about peasant revolutions. His idea of becoming a priest was now transformed into an urge to help the peasantry. He often spoke to me of the Naxalite movement, which was inspired by Mao's idea of peasant-led revolutionary war. In 1973 he went to Coimbatore to work for a water and agricultural development, and to dig wells for peasants who had no water. He earned 800 rupees a month, instead of 3,000 ...

Vincent was at first a little angry; but also proud of his son. 'Peter's like that. He's always wanted to do something for the poor, and talking with you has made him even more so inclined.' Again I feel the implacable web, the strands that are now knitting us together, binding us to each other. Yes, we had talked, Peter and I. As I had talked also to Appa, about the need for the infrastructure of water in the countryside, for canals and reservoirs and wells; and about how, because of Mao Zedong, half of China's arable land was in the process of getting stable irrigation. I hear Peter say: 'It's because of you ... because of you that I was sent to Europe, and then I came back to dig wells, and then I went to Iran and became sick ... ' I interfered, without wanting to. Sometimes I feel almost as if I were guilty ...

In 1971, Vincent's divorce was duly pronounced and we went through a brief ceremony in Appa's house in that April. The lawyer came, and it was all over in five minutes. A marriage not church-recognized, not publicized, and since then, even Vincent has wondered, twice, whether it was a 'proper marriage'. That is something he says when he becomes, suddenly, very 'Catholic', and unhappy. But I do not hurt easily. I laugh and say: 'Oh, it'll grow on you, it'll grow. It's an English common-law marriage.' It is Peter who can say things that hurt, not Vincent.

Appa was present at our wedding, dressed in his best Nehru jacket. Appa, beaming benignly at me, and afterwards coming to me shyly, to put a hand on my sleeve, and to nod his head. 'This is a joyful occasion for me,' Appa said. And that was total acceptance. Aggie came up to hug me, and called me sister, and so did Theresa and Cissy. And so, in the end, I did acquire an Indian family. No small affair, to be an Indian daughter-in-law, in an Indian Catholic family.

I was to attend many family weddings later. And of course mine was very different. There were so few people present; only the immediate family circle, three sisters and two brothers. Not like when a 'real' wedding is celebrated, and all the relatives come, and we sit down 400 at table, if not more...

After the lawyer had departed there was a very nice meal. The sisters overdid themselves; the brothers all tried their best. The Family are excellent trencher-men, and the quantities of food – curds, chicken Masala, mutton curry, fish, rice, *chapatis* – that they can put away is quite wonderful to behold.

In that year, however, brother Dominic began to have his first heart symptoms. He was a debonair, cheerful man, who had always been most hospitable to me, although he insisted on calling the border conflict 'the Chinese invasion'. He was now on a diet of his own contrivance which, calorie-wise, was no less, but perhaps a little more, than what he was in the habit of consuming.

By 1970 relations between India and China were changing.
It was in 1970 that the Chinese ambassador in Paris first
suggested that Vincent should go to China. This was
surprising; but even more surprising was the fact that the
Indian government immediately issued Vincent with a
valid passport for China ... so that he became the first Indian
in almost ten years to travel to China, with official blessing.

In Beijing, Prime Minister Zhou Enlai gave both of us an
important interview, and talked at length with Vincent
about the border problem between the two countries. I was
happy that Vincent was sharing with me this unique experience: meeting the man who, through the havoc and turmoil
of the Cultural Revolution, kept steady, kept things working, and saved so many people's lives. During those years, I
felt that Zhou Enlai, for the sake of keeping China together,
sacrificed himself and asked all of us (of course, without
saying so) also to do nothing to endanger the process he was
trying to push through, and which was still so frail: the
opening up of China, and the resumption of relations with
America.

Improving relations with India was but one aspect of this
total situation; and in 1971 I was again in China, and then in
India, where I also had meetings with Indira Gandhi, the
late Prime Minister of India, on the India–China situation.

During these years Peter, after turning down the job with
Tata, was continuing to dig wells in Coimbatore, a fairly
arid region in South India. A cousin of the family also lived
there; she was a teacher, a charming woman, and seemed to
care a great deal for Peter. But again Peter could not make
up his mind. He did surface once in Madras, however, at the
time of Poon Puhar, the Feast of Abundance, or Harvest
Festival; an occasion for joyous processions, taking out the
chariots of the gods, and bazaars, and dancing and singing.
Peter talked to me again about the Naxalites. He was
indignant at the rural distress, and tempted to join this

52

peasant revolt. But I felt it was something he would not carry through. It had no chance of success within the powerful structure of repression which exists in India, which had been much stronger than that in China before the Revolution.

'India has fourteen major languages and they are a barrier to any overall revolt,' I said to Peter. 'A general insurrection was successful with Gandhi, because there was a common cause, independence. But a peasant revolt will encounter the obstacles of not only the police and army, but also of religion and caste.'

Peter began to write to me. He was now puzzled about the *rapprochement* between America and China. 'Why, why, you know that America is imperialist. Why is China making friends with America?'

How hard it was to explain to Peter, to make him accept that in international relations there are no angels and no devils, only complex and necessary compromises, alliances, national interests ... I think he felt that I was now contradicting myself.

'You talked against the Vietnam war ... now you're accepting to be friends with America,' he accused me.

'But, Peter, I've always been "friends", as you say. With the American people. That does not mean agreeing with all the policies of America ... '

He shook his head. To him, all this was almost immoral. Yet he felt that I was a person he could talk to about the world. Abruptly one day he said: 'I want to go into politics.'

'You? Politics? What will you do?'

'I want to make my country India better. I want to do something to help India.'

'You'll be doing a good deal and digging wells is quite admirable ... '

'Yes, but ... ' He told me the wells did some good, but in many areas the untouchables were not allowed to use them. Only the landlords. And if the untouchables displeased the landlord, then they got no water. However, in certain parts

53

of India, such as in the Punjab, the green revolution was beginning. More fertilizers, more mechanization. But, as a result, the proportion of landless peasantry was increasing as farms were rationalized. They came to the cities, surrounding them with belts of slums. In ten years, in Tamil Nadu alone, the proportion of the landless peasantry had increased from 20 to 40 per cent...

'But this is progress,' said Vincent, hard-headed. Progress undoubtedly. The quantity of grain produced began to increase, but I wondered whether the number of hungry was actually diminishing...

In August of 1975 Appa's ninetieth birthday anniversary was celebrated with great pomp in the city of Madras. A High Mass was held at the Cathedral of St Thomé. The Archbishop of Madras officiated. He chose for his sermon a long homily against the sins of the flesh, and against family planning. No one smiled. The Family, the relatives, all had come. The church was filled. Theresa counted 470 of them (not including the babies).

After Mass, Appa and I left together (me by his side, as Eldest Daughter-in-law, though my status still seemed very dubious to many of the relatives, still under the shock of such un-Catholic goings-on). Appa said, in a little aside to me: 'I do not feel the sermon was quite appropriate in my case.' He twinkled, full of fun, then turned to lead the throng of relatives across to the house in San Thomé Road where he had lived for so many years. Thence, for lunch, we adjourned to a public hall, hired for the purpose, large enough to contain the crowd. The women wore their most gorgeous saris, the young girls all had sprays of blossom tucked in their hair. The men stood in groups or came up one after the other, filing by to 'wish' Appa. The term 'to wish' in Indian-English means to greet, to congratulate, to come up to shake hands and say good morning. It means acknowledgment of one's presence. Indians are great experts in being able to convey total ignorance of your

54

physical presence, as anyone who has waited in front of an official, while he is writing something, or reading something, not looking up at all at the figure standing in front of him, can testify.

'All the Royapuram crowd is here,' said Theresa to me. She was coping with the usual family squabbles as regards seating at the long tables; the distance in metres from Appa was a matter of great concern. It is easy to insult an Indian relative. 'I should have been fourth on the table on the right,' I heard someone shout. 'Instead Theresa has put so-and-so in my place because, of course...' Family memories, family grievances, family history dating back, back...

But decorum, good manners, would prevent major outbursts. And then, before lunch was served, there was a prayer, and Appa's smallest great-grandchild, Prathap, was lifted up to garland the old man with a big wreath of flowers.

I love those crowds of Asia. I love the feeling of deep sea diving it gives one to lose oneself in a multitude, good-natured and jostling. Out of it comes a kind of trance, an initiation into another consciousness of body. So I tried to lose myself in that vigorous, moving, colourful throng as they moved in and out. But it could not be. I was different, and was *someone* (even if the very epitome of Sin), and some must have wondered how Appa, President of the Catholic Association of India, had condoned his eldest son's misbehaviour...besides that, I was the only one in cotton shirt and skirt in the heat of August, everyone else sweating gently, muskily, in their best Kanchipuram saris of heavy silk. I told Appa how much I loved crowds and he was a little puzzled. For he, a great progenitor, having engendered eleven sons and daughters, of whom nine were alive, had always preferred the company of books to the company of people.

'Do you? I had imagined that you would like to be alone, at times...'

'At times, yes, but then I get hungry for human contact. What the French call *un bain de foules*. It's invigorating.'

I later sat with another relative, Miss Doraisamy, bony, nervy, thin, with enormous eyes in a thin face. She painted, in a room in a house whose walls oozed with convention, propriety, Catholicism. She lived in Royapuram, and was not married because she preferred painting. Great odd slashes of colour, things unconventional. She fought against Indian film poster art, against the simpering flowers and kittens of English calendar art still prevalent in India, against the bibulous, elephantic, Indian representational religious art... She had no money, no way of meeting other painters, no possibility of buying art books from the West. But she painted ... and she was helpless. For being without a husband, her brothers might one day bully her out of her inheritance – one-third of the house. And deprived of a house, what would she do? But she painted...

So many lives, so many secret stories, secret but open, as in family reunions the women come together in the long drowsy afternoon, while the men scatter, go for walks, disappear, and the women remain, seated on borrowed chairs, or lying, several together on a mat or a bed – resting and talking or not talking, waiting for sundown, and perhaps then a bath and a change of sari before the evening feast. Sundown, when the more energetic and their children will go for a walk by the beach. For then the stifling, still afternoon is over, giving place to the sea wind, along the marvellous ocean shore just in front of the cathedral of Mylapore, along the eight kilometre-long ocean shore and its white-gold sand ... Life is rich then with episodes, little things, disembodied words which linger in the air. I sat, unobtrusive, among the women, without trying to talk. Silence is so important, and an air of lassitude. So that even the most pious of step-aunts by marriage seemed mollified. I listened, listened to the waves of sound, the rhythms of Indian-English, Tamil-English, one of the numerous Englishes which have been created out of English. Or listened just to plain Tamil, that extraordinarily musical language which requires an extreme agility of tongue and reminds one of the rumbling ocean waves of Madras... Pity that Peter was not there. The sheer bliss of swimming in a strange sea of other human beings, other voices... he had not come to the celebration of his grandfather's ninetieth birthday. But then Peter disliked all ceremonies, weddings; he would not attend his sister's wedding...

That night there were more polite arguments under the red- and gold-roofed tent Theresa had erected in the garden, while great plates of steaming rice, fragrant with cloves and other spices, and meats were circulated. Some relatives threatened to go home; youngsters were sent to get conveyances – tri-motors or trishaws. Clusters of women swayed in the semi-darkness, with that particular water grace of movement of the South Indian women, and did not speak to each other; oh, it was quite a *tamasha*, a bash-up, said Cissy. The men congregated round the rain tree, and were finally dragged away by their respective families. Benny and Cissy swore they would never again speak to so-and-so...

Appa's ninetieth birthday was indeed a wonderful event. It lasted three days, with times for siesta, and even for television. Another event was a dinner, given by the state governor, attended by Madras officials, and some *chettiars* or money-lenders, described in Indian-English as 'prominent in their gifts to Education', and local politicians. Appa rose to make a speech.

'We have forgotten the Indian peasant,' he said. And spoke of the 120 million, the untouchables, still held in bondage as slaves; of debt bondage; of children whose lives were no better than, as he put it, the beasts of the field. There was some discomfort among the politicians, but they quickly recovered, and unctuous phrases rolled out of them, each one professing total dedication to 'the uplift of the weaker sections of our society'.

Soporose, we went home, where I was immediately

struck with food poisoning and lay prostrate for the next two days. When I left I held Appa's hand and told him how wonderful it had been to be present on his ninetieth birthday. He shook his head. 'So much money spent,' he said. 'It could have been given to those who need it.' That is how it was with Appa.

Peter had missed all these days of ceremony, eating, and quarrelling, and rejoicing, and children yelling, of garlanding Appa, of bursts of laughter, of tears among the women, of sari-changing three times a day, of showing off one's jewellery ... Of men huddling in groups, holding glasses of the local rum or beer in their hands and gazing unblinkingly in front of them; most of them handsome, all of them extremely courteous. Letting the women (Theresa especially, who is at her best when coping with several hundred guests) perform the tribal interplay of agreement and quarrel, of love and resentment ... all of it necessary to weave the family web. For three days Vincent and Theresa supervised, checked, commandeered, sent off people in all directions to see to the food, the drinks, the chairs, the glasses, the rum, the ice ... also to see that the servants had their share.

'Vincent, why isn't Peter here?'

'He's too serious about his work.'

'But he also didn't turn up for Patricia's wedding ... '

Patricia – courted by a most handsome young man, a Hindu, of a Brahmin family. It was a love marriage, and the bridegroom's family, despite some tut-tutting aunts, had agreed. There had been three ceremonies: a Catholic Mass at the church in Bangalore; a Hindu ceremony, where Patricia had changed saris several times, and worn a belt of solid twenty-two-carat gold round her waist. The gifts had filled two rooms in the bridegroom's parents' house. Then there had been a civil ceremony, and a big reception at the Bangalore Club (around 500 guests). Patricia's mother, Caro, was there, as I was. We became friends on that occasion. An unenforcedly happy marriage. Peter had not come.

'Peter has always been like that,' says Michael. And that is that.

Appa moved to stay with his youngest daughter Aggie, who had married her first cousin on her mother's side, Patrick, just as her sister Rina had married Patrick's brother. Appa complained that the bus which stopped in front of the old house made too much noise, and so withdrew to the apartment in Foreshore Estate, which was much quieter, although far less spacious. It was curious that Appa would suddenly get so sensitive to noise, since he had appeared to me totally unaware of voices, children's laughter, screams; but move he did.

The Foreshore Estate was a series of buildings, each of them containing apartments, built upon a wide expanse of sand by the government for what was called the Middle Income Group (M.I.G.) of civil servants. The rents were controlled, and because Appa stayed there a telephone was installed. It is very hard to obtain a telephone in Madras. Or in Bangalore. I believe that the period of waiting, normally, is round twelve years. Unless, of course, one has pull, or knows someone who knows someone in the P.T.T. (Post, Telegraph, Telephones), or there is a need for a telephone. Appa, as a member of the Rajya Sabah, and eminent, could of course get a telephone easily. Scholars and pundits, students of various kinds, some of them Americans, came to see him at Foreshore Estate. His eyes bright, his mind clear, Appa would sit in the tiny 'living room' facing the outside door, where an overhead fan whirled, at times dizzily. He was also planning another book; the last one, his eighth, he had finished when he was eighty-eight years old.

Because, after Appa's birthday, I was extremely busy, I lost sight of Peter for a while, but not for very long. He would emerge from digging wells in South India, and be back in Belgium with Freddi Dahlmann and his company in Charleroi. Freddi had not forgotten Peter. 'He is a very good engineer, your Peter. We would be glad to have him back.' There was a need for engineers in Libya. An electric power station was to be built in that country. 'Moamar Gadhafi is of course quite mad and they don't like white people there,' said Freddi. Peter, with his Portuguese-Indian looks, would attract less hostility.

Peter came to see me in Switzerland, at my apartment in Lausanne, on his way to Belgium. Vincent and he had long talks in the study. Vincent was trying to persuade Peter to accept the Libya job. Peter and I walked by the lake, and talked about Libya.

'I expect you'll find it difficult but interesting, Peter.'

He turned to me. 'I feel I'm letting down the poor people, Suyin. Once again I'm going to have a well-paid job. Abroad.'

'But you have now done what you could, Peter... for some years. Even if you spent a lifetime digging wells, it wouldn't make all that much difference.'

'So you think Daddy is right?'

'I think he's trying to make you into a success... yes, I also think you'll be able to build bigger things than wells, after this job.'

He thought a little, and I knew it was hard for him to think that personal success would not be exploitation.

'Peter, look. In China we don't believe in too much asceticism. It's not by depriving yourself that you're going to save the world.'

Peter went off to Libya. But I was a little uneasy. I had been glib, explaining away, too easily, that aspiration of his. Soothing his scrupulous, admirable conscience. Perhaps he was just on the point of giving all of himself, in total dedication. And perhaps not, being the forever hesitant person he was. Perhaps Vincent and I had deflected him from his course, which was, actually, a search for some kind of sainthood. I had interfered in his destiny... Karma.

Flims was beautiful, with thick, two-metre-high snow; the Dahlmanns came, exuberantly, and we had wonderful parties with them and nightly bridge sessions with Freddi and his beautiful wife, Lisi. They were a boisterous crowd and Peter came to visit us, and joined in the fun. He brought for me a white wool burnous from Libya. We went climbing, some of us went skiing, I walked for hours in the snow.

Peter luged down a mountain with a party, and so did I, happily whizzing on the sinuous path among the pines. When we returned home, Peter discovered that he had lost his keys. Keys to his home in Libya, keys to his files, perhaps. The next day he retraced, on foot, the way we had come, going over every foot of the mountain path, and found his keys in the snow. He had gone about the search with the same tenacity and method with which he tackled everything, and it had taken him seven hours.

We went bowling. We went tramping in the snow, trying to discover a small lake I had seen in the forest; but with the muffling white thickness of snow overwhelming all land-marks I lost my sense of orientation. Snow all about; and only the forest of spearlike pines, everywhere. Finally we fell, not upon the lake, but into a small ravine. Peter picked himself up, brushing his coat. A pine tree abruptly unloaded upon him a small avalanche of snow and this made him happy. We came home, where Vincent, who does not like tramping, was cooking a curry, the apartment redolent of Indian spices. Happy days. Peter looked so well, contented. He did not talk much of Libya; as usual it was question, question, and very short answers. But he did manage to tell me that the engineers lived quite apart from the local people. 'Gadhafi is very religious, he does not drink, he works hard.' As usual, there seemed a blankness. The blanket of blankness Peter wraps around himself while he thinks, thinks ... trying to make up his vacillating mind.

'Peter, write to me. Let me know how you get on in Libya.'

In that tight, low voice of his which is Peter's when he tries to conceal all emotion, he said:

'You write to me too. Don't forget.'

V

In China, the popular premier, Zhou Enlai, still today called 'the well-beloved', died in January 1976 and Mao Zedong died in that September. A month after Mao's death his wife and her supporters, the notorious Gang of Four, were brought down, and thus ended the harrowing ten years of the Cultural Revolution.

Now it was possible for me to do something about my own family in China. I had, precariously and with a great deal of anxiety, tried to alleviate their plight. But since the very fact that I was 'an outside connection', which meant living outside China, and not fully Chinese, was harmful to them, I had had to be very careful. As had many thousands of other people who had relatives, Overseas Chinese, abroad. Some of the harrowing experiences of my relatives I shall not relate here; I was quite unable to talk about them, for talking, especially abroad, where the press might pick up these stories, was itself dangerous to their lives. There was, during the years of the Cultural Revolution, a gap between the 'top' and the mid-level in the Party bureaucrats. While at the 'top' certain people, such as myself, seemed welcome (although very carefully watched), my relatives were constantly being hauled up to reveal what they had said to me.

I now had to return, and help get them back into their jobs; help them get their salaries paid to them. I also had many friends I had looked after during those years (simply by telling the bureaucrats how ardently they supported whatever was happening, because anything else might have jeopardized their lives). These friends were grateful to me. Now I could help them a little more. I would invite some of them to go abroad. Others I would be able to see reinstalled in their former positions, and amply compensated.

I returned in April 1977 from China, and passed through India, on my way back to Switzerland, to see Appa. Vincent had stayed with his father, who was becoming weaker. He moved very little, and slowly. He would be ninety-two in August of 1977.

A short while after we left India to return to Lausanne, Appa slipped on the bathroom floor and broke his hip bone. He lay in bed for about three weeks, and died in his sleep, in June.

Vincent and I were told the news by telephone, and also that burial would take place within twenty-four hours, because of the heat, the impossibility of keeping the body in the house. Vincent flew to India as soon as he could; he was, as eldest son, entrusted with the execution of his father's will. There was a solemn Mass held in memory of Appa in July.

And in that summer Dominic, Vincent's younger brother, had another heart attack (his third). He lingered in hospital for some weeks, and died. Vincent now had to attend to other business matters, as well as to help his brother's widow.

I mourned Appa, whom I had dearly loved. But precisely in that summer I had many Chinese friends coming abroad, and some staying with me. It was the first time in many years that they had been outside China, and I had to look after them. I knew that Appa would not care whether I attended a solemn Mass for him or not; genuine love is not dependent on such outward manifestations of emotion. His affection for me, totally unflawed, was with me always. There was about his death a kind of aptness, which made grief artificial. Appa had died without pain; I had a photograph of him and myself, laughing together, taken just a few months before he died.

In the winter of 1976-7 Peter had returned from Libya for a holiday in India. It appears that, during those months in India, he complained of severe headaches, which were ascribed to a long-standing sinus infection, and for which he seems to have been given massive doses of antibiotics. He was now being assigned as an engineer for a project in Iran, connected with a large power station to be built there. It was a job with responsibility and a good salary. He wrote to me, saying that he looked forward to being in Iran. He went from India to Teheran, and wrote me two letters, to which I answered. In July, he rang me up from Teheran.

'Tell me, Suyin, what do you think of the Shah?'

I laughed. 'Not on the telephone, Peter, please. How are you?'

'Not bad. I have some headaches, that's all.'

'Your father's in India. I think the commemoration Mass is taking place this month.'

'Yes, Daddy told me.' Peter paused. 'I don't like all those ... ceremonies,' he said.

'I too can live without them, but they're necessary.' I laughed. 'Peter, you don't like weddings, funerals ... take care to be there at your own wedding, Peter.'

He did not laugh. I turned to the Chinese friends who were staying with me. 'My stepson asks me what I think of the Shah,' I said in Chinese. 'And on the telephone. The Shah's police are probably listening.'

There was at that time, in Europe, a campaign against the Shah, against his persecution of dissidents. Iranian students in India, in France, held demonstrations against him. The Ayatollah Khomeini was being given asylum in France.

I wondered what was really going to happen in Iran. Peter, as I knew, was engaged on a project which would have made it possible for Iran to industrialize swiftly, using its own oil. This would have been beneficial to the country. The Shah was pushing through reforms, pushing through the industrialization of Iran. He was pushing much too hard, and he was surrounded by corrupt men, he did not have competent people to run the country. Did someone, somewhere, surmise that if the Shah were successful this would be a threat to the total control, by the multinationals, of Iran, and of the oil-bearing countries? Should Iran become a powerhouse of industry, having such potential by processing its own oil, and by forcing the pace of progress, it might become a power among the Arab states. Perhaps the whole situation in the Middle East would then change. True, the Shah was a tyrant, a dictator ... but there were far worse ones than he. The indignation suddenly generated in the West against the Shah was somewhat puzzling to me. And the favour shown to the Ayatollah Khomeini in France was also difficult to understand.

I wrote to Peter: 'You've asked me what I think of the Shah. I think he's rushing things too much. Dispossessing landlords, cutting down the power of religious communities. He's got corrupt people around him. He hasn't got a civil service competent to carry out the reforms he's madly pushing through ... '

Peter received my letter, for he mentions it in the last letter he wrote to his father, dated July 12, 1977, when Vincent was in India.

Dear Daddy,

Thank you for your letters of the 4th and 25th of June. I did write to you at Lausanne. Suyin must have sent the letters to you.

First my condolences to you and all the children on the

demise of your father [sic]. I am sorry not to be able to be there for the memorial Mass on July 30 and the other ceremonies.

I was agreeably surprised to receive a letter from Suyin some days ago and am in the process of replying to it.

The sinus has started troubling me again. It was bad, especially when I was in India. Have been to see a doctor here who put me on a massive course of antibiotics which helped. Took an X-ray after and it did not show anything. But I still get the headaches and fever ...

This is the only letter, to his father, in which Peter ever wrote of his headaches. I had opened the envelope, to send the contents, airmail, to Vincent in Madras.

Another problem had to be faced. Aggie and Patrick's son, Thomas, had muscular dystrophy. I remember the equable, tranquil manner in which Patricia told me during my brief visit. An indifference of expression, which is deceptive; all emotion internalized. I had also seen Aggie, who had been told by the doctor what the outcome would be. 'It's God's will,' said Patrick. He too appeared, as Aggie did, entirely calm. They prayed, fervently, but quietly. They trusted God. Patrick had asked me whether there was any hope of a cure. I told him that a lot of people were trying to find one, that there was an association for muscular dystrophy in America. 'Oh, do *Americans* also get it?' asked Patrick. To him, it seemed Americans must be invulnerable to such defects. I told him it spared no one. Someone had hinted that Thomas's condition might be the result of consanguineous marriage. Anne, Michael's wife, had told me that most of the mentally backward in the school where she worked were the result of 'first cousin marriages'. 'It's all due to caste. Caste makes it sometimes impossible to marry anyone except within a very narrow environment, and as you know, Suyin, ninety-nine per cent of Indian marriages are arranged by the parents.' She was a little smug about it, feeling proud that, in her case, it had not been so; her marriage to Michael had been a love marriage. For as an Anglo-Indian, also with French and Portuguese ancestors (she was very proud of a French piratic great-grandfather, a romantic hero with blue-green eyes which had been inherited by her third son), Anne had really escaped the caste system, and felt far removed from the danger of genetic quirks.

But should Aggie and Patrick come to believe that it was their 'first cousin marriage' which had led to the congenital defect in their only son Thomas, it would wreck them, burden them with a guilt for which they were not responsible. And it was also untrue; for many muscular dystrophies occur in the offspring of people totally unrelated by consanguinity. I talked with Patrick about it, and reassured him that it had nothing to do with his being Aggie's first cousin. It is the most frightful burden of all to bear an 'original sin' – the steady unrelenting pressure of guilt, daily, hourly. And upon innocents. And not even scientifically correct. I hoped that Anne's theories would not seep into the Family. They were banal, belonging to the category of modern superstition. And now Aggie and Patrick were to have no more children; for fear that, should they produce another son, another accident might happen. And they were Catholics, fervently so. No birth control pills or other mechanical aids.

We were due, Vincent and I, to go to China that year of 1977. In late August. I had much to do there, notably to speed up the rehabilitation of my relatives. There was the matter of getting the accusation of 'landlord class', which had been affixed upon my Third Aunt, lifted. I had to get Sixth Brother, my cousin (but in China all first cousins are called brother and sister), to come out of China for a tour of the West. He was chief engineer for telecommunications in our province of Sichuan (only around 100 million people who would need telephones one day), and I felt that telecommunications was of decisive importance for techno-logical advance in China. That, and transport, and energy. I

68

had relatives in radar, in laser techniques ... all my family in China are scientists, and they had a very hard time during the Cultural Revolution. Now that it was over, there was so much to do, and I was involved, part of it all. Part of the Renaissance in China. From many friends came letters asking for help, now that it was no longer so dangerous to be my friend. I had also accepted, in 1976, an invitation for a comprehensive lecture tour in Canada, and also to some universities in the United States, which were puzzled by the upheavals in China. I had a photography book on China coming out, as well as a book on Tibet, since I had been to Tibet (the first person admitted there in almost twenty years) in late 1975. And I was finishing a book to wind up my own autobiography. While Appa's death in India had been peaceful, family-surrounded, my beloved Third Uncle in China had died alone. His son, his daughter-in-law, had not been allowed to come to see him as he lay in bed, in his last agony. His wife, Third Aunt, accused of being 'landlord descendant', had been following re-education classes, and was only allowed to be with him at night. Even today, no one knows where Third Uncle's corpse lies buried. For 'capitalists' such as he – my family, after all, was a pioneer family in introducing railways and industry to China way back in the early twentieth century – nothing was bad enough, in those havoc days of the Cultural Revolution. Third Uncle died in 1968; it was only in 1985 that his son, my Sixth Brother, told me (with that bitter laugh which is the Chinese opposite of mirth) that, panicked at the thought that I might come and demand to see his grave, the lower Party cadres of the Cultural Revolution unit had hastily built a fake tombstone for him. But lo and behold, being a person with some sixth sense, I had not asked to see his grave, because I knew that, at times, in the havoc and tumult of enormous proportion which beset nations and peoples, it is better to let matters go, not to ask, not to demand, merely to wait ...

But now a change had come; everything that had been

badly done, every injury done to any person in China, would now be repaired. And it fell upon me, in that autumn of 1977, to do what I could for my own family, my own friends. This involved parleys, meetings, circumlocutory banquets where a casual phrase means more than all the speeches made. For that is the Chinese way. Treading lightly and delicately, with polite smiles upon my face (always smile, in Asia, especially when you are extremely upset and digging for facts), I would go round, and here and there in the middle of eulogy and placebic phrases would drop a hint. I was also booked now to give lectures in China, at teachers' colleges and at universities.

With all this upon me, the least of my worries should have been Peter, Peter who in that summer had written a few lines to me. 'Thank you for your letter. I am getting on well, except that my sinuses are troubling me ... '

Retrospectively, reading his earlier letter to his father, I am puzzled. Why, bizarrely, did Peter write 'the children' to his father, meaning his own brother and sister? Why 'condolences', except that the word is used every time, formally, in that staid, Victorian Indian-English employed in India and which denotes 'good breeding'? Why this extraordinary detachment from his own grandfather? As if he was out of it all, not participating, as if it had nothing to do with him. Perhaps it was part of his own personality; but perhaps, also, it was a herald of his sickness.

On the afternoon of August 4, I was putting the finishing touches to a chapter, and Cecile, a French friend of mine, had come to stay with me. My Sixth Brother was also staying, and another Chinese friend had been put up in a hotel nearby. The telephone rang. It was Niels Dahlmann, the eldest son of Freddi Dahlmann, ringing from Brussels.

'Suyin, it seems Peter is not well. He seems to have collapsed at work, in Teheran. Probably the heat ... don't worry, our company is sending out a doctor for him. We might evacuate him to Belgium. I don't think the doctors are very good in Teheran.'

'I'll try to get Vincent, Niels. He's in India at the moment, arranging things for the Family because his father and his brother both died recently.'

'Don't worry, we're doing all we can,' said Niels. I spent some hours on the telephone. I tried to get Vincent. I do not quite remember what was wrong at the time. The telephone to India kept on humming, emptily. I sent cables. To Bangalore. To Madras. Where the hell was he? Perhaps he had gone with the Family on a pilgrimage. Pilgrimages to the shrine of the Holy Virgin Mary, so popular in South India that even Hindus join in worshipping her. A mother goddess. Maybe he was elsewhere, or playing rummy. Maybe ... Finally, I did reach Michael in Bangalore on the second day and relayed to him the news of Peter's illness. 'Tell your father to ring me up as soon as possible.' Michael said that Vincent was in Bombay, with Patricia.

Vincent rang me from Bombay. 'But I cannot buy a ticket without foreign exchange,' he said. The problem was that we had bought our tickets to Hong Kong, in order to go to China in late August, together; but now he had to rush back to Europe, and he had not carried with him any foreign money. In India, control over the rupee is very strict; it is not possible to buy an airline ticket to places outside India without foreign exchange.

I rushed to get the airline ticket; but there was another difficulty. Vincent has kept his Indian passport. He refuses to change. 'I am Indian, I have an Indian passport.' But Indian passports need visas for other countries; and Vincent had to go to Delhi to get a Belgian visa, from the Belgian embassy there. The visa would take a minimum of twenty-four hours to process. Meanwhile, Niels kept in touch with me. A woman doctor, Dr Beckers, had flown to Teheran to retrieve Peter. Peter had been placed in a hospital in Teheran, and, suspecting meningitis, a spinal puncture had been done on him. The result was dubious. Dr Beckers had to get him out of hospital. Had to book seats on a plane from Teheran to Brussels. But planes from Teheran are not terribly efficient; it took them twenty hours to reach Brussels. Peter was placed in a private room in the prestigious Hôpital St Pierre, one of the best in Europe.

'Don't worry, we've got the best doctors to look after him,' said Niels. By then it was August 9.

Vincent flew to Brussels to be with his son. Peter was coherent, he spoke to his father. Dr Beckers reported that he had been rather somnolent on the plane, complaining of headache. He had a slight temperature. Vincent rang me up to say that he seemed all right. 'They don't quite know what it is,' he said. 'They think it might be malaria.'

'He's had sinus trouble ... it may be a brain abscess. I've seen one, in Hong Kong,' I said.

'They're doing all the examinations, for all tropical diseases too, including malaria, everything. He's very thin ... He's worked too hard and neglected himself.'

Brain abscess; meningitis ... my mind kept on working on this item. But it would be rash for me to try to diagnose from afar. One of the tenets of medicine that had been ground into me was: never, never try to treat your own family. But the idea of a brain abscess kept worrying me. 'And possibly Peter has been taking antibiotics for a long time for his sinuses ... antibiotics are unsafe, often out of date, often taken without any doctor's prescription ... tell the doctor all this, Vincent.'

Then for a while I debated whether I should fly to Brussels myself, to see Peter. But what could I do? Now I blame myself. Perhaps, perhaps, through some intuition, I would have hit on the right diagnosis, by fluke ... But by then Vincent, who had stayed five days in Brussels, was returning to Lausanne. Peter was feeling better, he said. He was having a lot of examinations. Niels and Freddi Dahlmann reassured us. 'He's got the best doctors we can get,' repeated Freddi. 'Leave him to us, he's like my own son to me.' Peter was having brain scans, X-rays, blood tests ... The company cared most handsomely for its engineers. 'No expenses spared, haha!' laughed Freddi.

I spoke to the doctor. There was indeed, he said, a suspicion of bacterial meningitis; and Peter had had a lumbar puncture in Teheran. He had also had episodes of amoebic dysentery ...

Our trip to China was not cancelled. I had to go anyway. Vincent was reassured. We would ring up from Beijing. Ring up Brussels every other day. Find out how things were with Peter. 'There is nothing to worry about,' repeated everyone, including the doctors.

By the time we left, on August 24, the daily bulletins by telephone reported Peter much improved; his fever had almost disappeared, and the antibiotics were stopped, as he was showing some signs of toxic reaction to them. I spoke with the doctor in charge on the telephone. 'Everything is under control,' said the physician. 'There does not seem to be anything radically wrong that we can find out.'

In Beijing, I was hectically busy. Every two days or so, we telephoned. Very often we could not speak to Peter himself, as he was 'having tests'.

On the afternoon of September 9 we rang Brussels again. The previous day we had had a cable from Niels that Peter was 'much better' and was soon to be discharged.

'Let's try to get Peter himself,' I said. It was not easy to reach him. But after hanging on for a fairly long time, Peter himself came on the line.

'Hello, Peter, I hear you're better,' I said. The line was quite clear.

'Suyin ... ' he said, 'I want to sleep.'

'Peter, we'll soon be seeing you.'

'Yes,' he said. And then: 'I am going to be discharged.'

I put the telephone down. His voice. His voice had altered! It was a strange, horribly strange, strangulated sound; it was not Peter's voice. It was a grinding, painful, slow dragging, as if a monstrous weight was being hauled. There was something terribly, terribly wrong. A wave of panic came over me. 'Vincent, I don't think Peter is at all

73

well; you must go to Brussels. I don't think he's well at all.'

Vincent had spoken to his son, saying: 'Hello Peter, how are you?'

'Hello, Daddy,' Peter had replied. And then he had put the telephone down.

Perhaps it was my intensity, perhaps it was Peter putting down the telephone, which made Vincent worried. He said: 'Why, what's wrong?'

'His voice. It's all wrong. Something is very wrong. I don't care what the doctors say, but Peter isn't well at all.'

'But Niels told us the hospital was discharging him.'

'But his voice. It's not normal. Maybe I'm silly, but I feel ... I feel you must go, you must. If he's being discharged, then you can bring him back to India. But something is wrong.'

And because of my intensity (which at times struck me as odd, foolish) everything began to move. That evening I asked my Chinese friends of the Friendship Association to arrange for a plane for Vincent from Beijing to Hong Kong. In Hong Kong Vincent would catch an Air-India plane to Europe.

The Chinese were splendidly helpful. They never questioned the reason why Vincent had to go, and all the travel plans within China had to be altered. They performed miracles, and a plane ticket was available on September 12. Thus, on that day, Vincent left Beijing for Hong Kong, India, Europe. It was, of course, my birthday. But since I do not celebrate my own birthdays, it did not matter. At times I thought: I'm making a fool of myself. And Vincent leaving me on my birthday was not quite what my Chinese friends and I had planned. For I was sixty that year, and everyone was planning a birthday party for me ... But I had told them: 'I feel something very bad is happening to my husband's son, but I cannot explain what it is. He had better go and see.'

On the morning of September 14 I received a cable, marked URGENT, from Niels: 'Peter has gone into a coma,

Vincent's presence urgently required.' Vincent? Where was Vincent? He should have caught an Air-India plane from Hong Kong. I rang up Bangalore, Madras, late at night. I got Patrick in Madras. Yes, Vincent was in Bombay... 'He's trying to get a plane,' said Patrick.

It took Vincent another day to reach Brussels, which he finally did on September 16. It was two more days before we could reach each other on the telephone. Peter was still in a coma, Vincent said. He had fallen into a coma just a day before he was to be discharged. 'But the doctors think there is a chance.'

'What do they say it is now?'

'They say it is tuberculous meningitis...'

Tuberculous meningitis. So common in India, so rare in Europe. Oh Peter, Peter, how the hell did you get tuberculous meningitis? And why was it not spotted? And the focus, the focus in the lung, probably, why was it not discovered?

I could not leave China without finishing all that I had to do. And there was so much to do. But in October, having attended to all my responsibilities, and having also seen my family, especially my Third Aunt, restored to her home, her 'surveillance' man, a worker, having now become a friend and saying: 'I always knew there was nothing wrong with the old lady', I flew back to Europe. I could not help thinking, on the way, of all my friends, my own cousins, my aunt, who had suffered for years. Some had died. Now Vincent had telephoned me from Brussels, saying that Peter was in a private room in the Hôpital St Pierre. My family had not had private rooms in hospital. My uncle had died because doctors were not keen on attending to the health of a 'capitalist'.

It was with a feeling of guilt, with a feeling that I was neglecting my Chinese family, my friends in China, for Peter, and for Peter because of Vincent, that I flew back. A divided mind, fragmented loves and loyalties... but I myself had formed that worldwide net of loves, of loyalties;

75

and I must treasure them all. All of them. I must always be available for anyone who wanted my help. I would not shrug away any tie, any burden. They were part of my life. They were me.

VI

Evil does not always come to do evil, says Incoronata, my Italian help, who once a week cleans my apartment in Lausanne. Such sentences sprout out of her effortlessly as grass grows in sunny weather. She was born in a poor village in southern Italy, where hunger was the normal accompaniment of her days, for many years. She remembers the babies crying of hunger; the huddled women exchanging words of comfort, acceptance. For who knows what God's will is towards His creatures? He inflicts evil upon them, but it must ultimately be for their good. Karma. Who can tell whether catastrophe is not, in the end, a blessing? Incoronata comforts me.

Peter lay in bed in the Hôpital St Pierre in Brussels. It was a wintry October, the cold afternoon sunlight touching every object with cruel clarity. A mocking small wind fingered my face. I thought, walking to the hospital: Love is not only a summer. Love has its winters too.

Vincent had now been in Brussels for several weeks; going daily at nine in the morning to the hospital and leaving at six at night. He was staying with Niels Dahlmann and his wife, who had taken him in without demur. Niels was very upset about Peter. 'I saw him and I wept,' he said. His eyes reddened at the memory. 'And when Peter went into coma, and we thought everything was over with him, I cried. Peter was quite special to all of us. He was so sweet, always so nice. He never said very much, but we all loved him.'

Peter lay in a coma when Vincent reached him from India, entirely bereft of response to sensation. Vincent sat down by his bed, and began speaking to him. Every day, for about three weeks, Vincent would speak to him from 9 a.m. to 6 p.m. He would assist the nurses in turning Peter, in tidying him. He spoke to him. Spoke to him. And towards the end of the second week he heard, from Peter, suddenly: 'Yes, Daddy.'

'Then I knew he would be all right,' Vincent said to me when I arrived. He was convinced that his son would pull through. Convinced that one day, one day, he would be as fit as ever. I could not warn him of the inevitable sequelae of tuberculous meningitis, the altered brain. He would not have listened.

'Come on, Peter, come on ... you must pull through this. You're strong, you're tough, Peter, you're going to make that effort, aren't you, master, aren't you ... I know you are ... you're getting better, Peter ... this is only a sickness, you mustn't let it beat you. Peter, I believe in you.'

Vincent. His presence, his warmth, his unfailing calling, calling to that battered brain of Peter's, pulling Peter out of that horror of non-being, trying to stir up Peter's own will, to overcome whatever had struck him. Life-giving warmth, presence, faith. Total faith in the power of love and of faith. I stood by the bed, and watched, and listened.

I consulted with the doctors. There was, and there would continue to be, in Peter, a resistance to being moved, being fed, being cleaned. He had exhibited this resistance from his first day in hospital. He fought silently, desperately, any

78

injection, any attempt to turn his body. He fought the urinary catheter and, unless watched, would pull out needles, catheter, everything. Until he went into coma. The medical extracts repeatedly note, before and after the coma period, this obstinate refusal of his to collaborate with the doctors.

Was this lack of co-operation due to his illness? Or to something preceding his illness? Was this stubbornness due to the anarchy in his brain, or part of his mental make-up, compounded in his consciousness a long, long time ago? I would not know. I still am not sure. I would suspect that a certain patient pliability, obedience, is almost demanded by physicians in the name of what is good for the patient; that resistance to medical care, to orders, upsets them. Perhaps this attitude of his also had to do with the delay which occurred in finding out what Peter really was suffering from. For, undoubtedly, there was some delay, as the chief physician himself, with great honesty, was to tell me. 'Unavoidable, due to the circumstances.'

The real diagnosis, tuberculous meningitis, was late by three weeks. Three unrecoverable weeks. The doctors cannot be blamed. The spinal puncture done in Teheran, which had 'revealed' a semi-purulent bacterial condition, masked for a good while the underlying tuberculous process. There were also other symptoms, which sent the doctors in charge puzzling over many diseases, and the X-rays did show something like an abscess formation in the cranial space. The low sugar in the cerebrospinal fluid might have been an early clue, but so far as I know, the laboratory tests at first did not show this. The bacterial infection of the central nervous system was treated with antibiotics, and on August 25, sixteen days after Peter's admission, he exhibited a toxic reaction to the drugs being used. They were stopped. That is when, clinically, Peter appeared better ... that is when the news, relayed by Niels, that he might soon be discharged, began to filter through to us in Beijing.

And then the doctor in charge was due for his annual holiday, and went away. Someone else came, who perhaps took it for granted that Peter's improvement was the end of the matter; that Peter's obstinate mutism was natural and pertaining to the fact that he was an Indian, in a foreign country. But very soon this assumption was shattered; the news that Peter was to be discharged was sent at the very time when the physicians began to suspect tuberculous meningitis. And in the second week of September another lung X-ray was performed (the first had appeared negative) and the small focus was discovered, behind the right clavicle. There had never been any cough or other symptoms of lung disease.

Just one unlucky thing after another, I thought, as I listened; and being a physician myself, knew how difficult the case must have been. 'We've never seen a case of tuberculous meningitis, not in the last twenty years,' the doctors would tell me. And when later in the year, while in New York, I mentioned Peter's case to a physician friend of mine, he corroborated this. 'We haven't had a case here for at least two decades, but of course in Latin America we do see them ... '

Confronted with this unfortunate multiplicity of infections, with the persistent sinus infection, and especially with that singular hostility of Peter's, his refractoriness to treatment, almost three weeks, if not more, of precious time were lost.

Peter then developed hydrocephalus; due to blockage by the thickened membranes wrapping the brain and the blockage of the ventricles within the brain. He was operated on, and a tube placed to drain the liquid into a blood vessel of the neck. He then developed septicaemia, and a urinary infection ...

September, October, November ... Vincent by his bedside every day.

'Come on, Peter, you'll fight this, you're going to fight this. We'll fight it together. Right, my son?'

80

'Yes, Daddy.'

'I want him home for Christmas,' Vincent said.

And of course Vincent was right. By early December, Peter was better. We had been told that during the Christmas holidays it would be difficult to give Peter all the attention he required. The hospital was very busy with urgent cases; and at that time of the year was chronically short-staffed. They tried to get ambulant patients home if possible. But he still needed hospitalization.

'We'll look after him at home over Christmas, then we'll see,' Vincent said.

From December 19 until January 4, 1978, the holiday season, Peter was with us. We flew him from Brussels to Geneva, and on by car to Lausanne.

From late October to late November, I had been in Canada on a lecture tour, arranged the year previously by the Canada–China Friendship Association. It was clear that I could not let them down. I lectured in a good many places in Canada, from Vancouver through Alberta and Saskatchewan to Quebec and Ontario. The Association could never have recouped the money they had spent hiring theatres and lecture halls and doing publicity for my tour. 'You must go,' Vincent said to me firmly. 'It's no use your staying here, it won't make Peter any better.'

Vincent would cope. It was a matter between him and his son now, and I knew that he wanted to pull Peter out of his sickness by his own efforts. It was something I could not interfere with. He had to do it in his own way. So off I went to Canada, thinking of Vincent, missing him, ringing long distance from every stop. Thirty below zero in Saskatchewan. A warm ten below in Toronto. I told my Canadian friends that Vincent had not been able to come because of his son's illness; several years later I would be faced with the rumour, begun at the time, that my husband had left me and that I was in the throes of a divorce. Perhaps because my temper – never anything but fierce – had been a little worse than usual. I am sure I did look worried. I do not remember a word of my lectures. I could not sleep well. But then, on lecture tours, some eager people do seem to think the lecturer needs neither food nor sleep. The Canada–China Friendship Association did all they could, however, to make me comfortable, and I still feel that, owing to Peter's illness, I did not quite come up to expectations on that tour.

Back then to Europe, and to the problem of Peter spending a Merry Christmas and a Happy New Year with us. After which he would again be hospitalized, this time in Switzerland. The physicians in Brussels told me the process of tuberculous infection was still in an active stage, something which later was confirmed, and that it might be difficult to handle Peter. 'I do not think he will ever be more than seventy per cent normal,' said the head physician. 'The usual sequelae of tuberculous meningitis, you know. But you may notice, suddenly, some improvement.'

On our return to Switzerland I went to investigate some clinics. And found that they took chronic cases, kept them under sedation. I went to the main hospital in Lausanne, and found a warm welcome. Yes, they would take Peter, but only on January 4.

'We'll manage.' I had no house help during those days; for my once-a-week cleaner took her holidays (skiing) from December 10 to January 10. I had not yet discovered Incoronata, my wonderful Italian cleaner, who understands what caring means.

Of those days I remember best, perhaps, my silliest worry: who was going to cope with Vincent's and Peter's shirts? For Vincent, being Indian, has never abandoned his habit of changing all his underwear, socks, and shirt, every day (and sometimes twice a day in hot weather). Now, if Peter was going to do the same, there would be a great pile of laundry for me ... these trivia do weigh heavily on a woman, especially a meticulous one.

There was a small problem of passports; Peter had to have a Swiss visa. The Swiss arranged it with utmost speed

82

('So long as all the bills are paid, of course he can come,' said the amiable comptroller of foreigners to me). There were some matters connected with Peter's insurance to settle, but apart from hospital expenses, Peter would have no great financial problem, and anyway Vincent and I were there to take care of that.

That Christmas and New Year were both awful and wonderful. Awful because we were both totally exhausted with the twenty-four-hour stint of caring for Peter. But not nerve-frayed; not pessimistic, not giving up. Only physically exhausted, because Peter had to be physically handled. We had bought special pants for him, since he could not manage his bowel movements. But he would not wear them. He continued in his obstinate unwillingness; he would continue when admitted later to the Lausanne hospital, where the doctors also found his 'negativeness' puzzling, as their reports indicate. 'He presents an opposi-tionism which makes any examination extremely diffi-cult ... by reason of his oppositionism and drowsiness, neurological examinations give little information ... '

Peter and Vincent slept in the twin beds in our bedroom. I slept in the spare room. Throughout the night Vincent would stay watchful; sometimes rise, to look at Peter, to straighten him from the intensely curled-up position he took. Vincent would get him up to pee, so that he would not wet the sheets. A shitting, peeing thirty-three-year-old is a bit of a problem. Peter once evacuated on my best 150-year-old Chinese rug. The rug took it very well; after I had cleaned it, it looked as good as ever, as if to say: 'I've seen worse during my lifetime.'

In the daytime we had to get him up, wash and shave him, and feed him. At first the feeding was a problem; Peter manoeuvred a spoon, but after a time was also able to deal with a fork, and a few weeks later with a knife. He did not slobber and did not take too big mouthfuls, but would at times stop eating, going into drowsiness again. It was really the toilet which was the greatest problem, as he would refuse to sit on the seat. He would spring up, and that was when there would be accidents, with smears all over the bathroom floor. But after a while Vincent knew how to deal with this, and would hold him down forcibly, for twenty minutes at a time, with occasional success. Peter refused to take his pills. Vincent would spend almost half an hour making him take his medicine, five times a day. We also made him walk. We took him out of the apartment, into the fresh air, because he paced the rooms, endlessly. And we talked to him. We even brought friends to talk to him, and he smiled, and said: 'Hello' and 'Good morning' and 'I'm better', so that we were much comforted. Because we felt quite exhausted, we tried to get a nurse for a couple of hours in the morning. The nurse came for three days, while I went shopping for food. She was a charming young woman, and liked Peter. 'Your son is so handsome, what a pity this has happened to him.' But after those three days she went off skiing (it was wonderful ski-weather in the mountains) and we could not get any more help. We had to remove all keys from their locks, for Peter would lock himself up in a room, or in the bathroom, and Vincent would stand outside the door, saying: 'Open, Peter, Peter, open ... ' and after about twenty minutes, sometimes longer, Peter would open, turning the key and letting Vincent in.

I noted that everything took so long to reach Peter's consciousness. One had to ask a question, then wait, then repeat it ... and after perhaps one, or two, minutes, he would begin an answer, then stop in the middle, because he had forgotten what he was about to say. This still happens to him, even now, some eight years later. But by dint of repetition, new paths of conduct, behaviour, control, understanding, memory, response, could perhaps be built up in his brain, or at least in that part of it which could be made to function, untraumatized.

'He'll be all right.' Vincent never wavered in his faith that one day, one day all would be well. To those of his friends who spoke of an institution he would say:

84

'We'll see.' Which of course meant no.

On January 4 the hospital in Lausanne admitted Peter. With Swiss thoroughness all examinations were again performed. The conclusion was that tuberculous activity was still present, still active. He remained in hospital until April 10, 1978. After the first three weeks we took him home at weekends, on Friday evening, returning him to hospital on Sunday evening.

Hospitals are reckoned efficient but impersonal. However, in Lausanne there was an excellent woman physician and a dedicated physiotherapist.

I would go to the hospital (Vincent was there, of course, every day, twice a day), and find one or the other of them talking with Peter … *talking*! Taking time to hear him mumble, taking time to be consoling, comforting. The physiotherapist expended a great amount of time and trouble on his limbs; and though at first Peter's obstructiveness made physiotherapy difficult, towards the end he began to like it. The drowsiness improved, but his way of silently fighting every attempt to make him take his pills, go to the toilet, wash, made the doctors envisage for a while some cerebral atrophy. He suffered from hypothermia, his limbs were cold and his blood pressure far below normal. Further tests were made for adrenalin deficiency. His walking, described as 'inebriate' since he staggered from side to side, would not become normal for some months. The male nurses at the hospital found him difficult; after a time they seem to have given up trying to bath him. When we fetched him home on Friday afternoons, Vincent would take off Peter's clothes, and his own, wrap a towel round himself, and begin the process of giving Peter a bath. During one of these bath sessions Vincent nearly fainted away, due to the moist heat and his own exertions, trying to hold Peter in the bathtub. 'I suddenly thought, suppose I get a heart attack and pass out, what would you do with Peter?' he said to me afterwards. Not a pleasant situation to contemplate.

85

There were times when it took both of us to get Peter to do simple things. At first, he could not put on his shoes and socks; he had to learn all over again. He hated, especially, having to wear those special pants, though he was unsafe without them. He would try to rip them off. He now had spells of frenzied activity alternating with drowsiness. At the hospital, he would not take his pills, and Vincent spent many hours trying to make him swallow his medicines. He became extremely constipated, which led a male nurse to the manual clearing of his rectum: painful but necessary. Laxatives made him not only uncomfortable but precarious. But after a time I could tell, when he returned to us at weekends, when he had an 'urge'. Like cats and babies, who become pensive or uneasy when their insides start gurgling, Peter would move his buttocks on his chair. I would say to Vincent: 'Let's try, he's got the urge.' Sometimes it worked, and sometimes not.

On April 10, 1978, the Swiss hospital discharged Peter. He was put on a maintenance diet of numerous pills; and we were given extracts of his medical history, so that he could be treated by other practitioners. Peter was much improved, said Vincent, though he still walked jerkily. His arms, however, were subject to spastic, uncontrolled movements. But he was now eating with a fork, and had almost given up fighting his father when washed. I had written to the physician in Brussels:

> There seems to have been a turning point ... Peter is more alert, and has regained some memory. He begins to show interest in what is happening. His left eye, his left hand, seem weak ... he still has urge incontinence, but is beginning to ask (by restless movement) for the toilet ... he goes up and down stairs without trouble ... his limbs are not so cold.

The Swiss physicians encouraged us. 'One never knows. It may take years, but he can continue to improve,' they said.

86

'We must stimulate other parts of his brain, parts which have not been diseased,' I said, half believing what I was saying, half not. The human brain is quite an extraordinary thing; there have been people in coma for months who were finally restored almost to normal ... The average person only uses one-tenth of his brain potential ... We knew there were other cases, elsewhere in the world. Other parents, fighting, never giving up; some of them in far worse economic situations than we were. Suddenly, I realized that, through Peter, I had achieved another penetration, into that world of parents, caring for the handicapped, invalids, morons ... and my heart went out to them. 'I know now what it is like,' I wanted to say to all of them, 'and what that daily martyrdom you endure so valiantly is like.'

I though often of Patrick and Aggie, their son little Thomas, such a handsome, cheerful little boy, suffering from muscular dystrophy, doomed to the slow death of all his muscles while his brain remained clear to the end.

Karma.

All over the world, in every country, there were parents whose offspring, through birth or disease or accident, were 'abnormal', or needed constant care. I saw them in Lausanne, getting out of a bus; the mentally deficient, the feeble-minded, from a special school. An energetic teacher, a young, pretty girl, was taking them to the zoo; she bounced and laughed, and cheered them on; not lethargic, loving her work.

And then there were the senile, the old people. A friend of mine, a secretary in an office, was looking after her old mother, who did not recognize her and struck at her with her cane when she tried to clean her, for she was totally incontinent. 'My sister and I look after her,' said the secretary. She earned for the three of them. And I met in Lausanne a woman taxi driver with a hemiplegic husband at home. Then there were parents coping with drug-addicted children ...

Perhaps, after all, Incoronata was right. Evil was not so

87

evil. Perhaps indeed Peter would recover ...

'I'll take Peter back to India, then we'll see,' said Vincent.

India, in its vastness, tolerates the handicapped, the misfits,
the insane. The latter sometimes become revered, being
'touched by God'. For India lives in two worlds – all of us
do, but do not acknowledge it – the so-called real, touch-
able, defined, confined to a meaning, and the unreal, fan-
tastic, dream world of the gods.

Peter would feel better, at home in India. Tuberculous
meningitis is so common in India, as all the Indian physicians we would consult told us. 'We have a hundred cases a
week,' one of them told me in Bombay. We had stayed once
with an Indian scholar, a scientist, Dr Mahalanobis, in his
house in Calcutta. And while we sat talking with him in the
living room, in came his wife, bursting with laughter. She
sat down, laughed again, and then left. 'She has had
tuberculous meningitis,' said her husband, very calmly, as
if that explained everything. There were servants to do all
the work, to take care of his wife. She never appeared again.
But she was home, and happy, even if unpredictable.

In India, we would find out what was the best way to help
Peter. At least we would not be so exhausted; we would
have servants, some help ...

On the plane, Peter was drowsy with pills but also had
sudden eruptions of ungovernable agitation. We kept his
belt on, which he resented. The staff of Air-India were
valiant; they rallied to help Vincent, they reasoned with
Peter when Vincent took him to the toilet. It was a struggle
all the way, but when he arrived in Bombay Peter said:
'We're going home, Daddy.' And to him home meant
Bangalore.

The Bangalore house, remodelled by Vincent, with two
floors and a large garden, was very comfortable. The top
floor was rented to a company. Michael and Anne and their
three children lived on the lower floor, where there were
three bedrooms, three bathrooms, a living room and a

dining room. Vincent had furnished it well; and there were also framed Chinese embroideries on the walls. Anne and Vincent had conflicting opinions about certain details, however. Anne liked doilies; she put doilies under everything. Vincent could never bear knick-knacks, doilies, coy gadgetry, porcelain dogs and shepherdesses. This at first did not seem to matter; for Anne and Michael were determined to help all they could with Peter. Michael especially devoted himself, in the first few months, to helping his father in getting Peter up, washing him, and feeding him. Peter always ate with us, although at times it was quite a strain, as he would shout, and get up to pace the room. But this was the only way for him to continue relearning, to be incorporated, once again, within a normal behaviour pattern.

The physician we were referred to was an expert in tuberculous meningitis. 'Had the patient been in India, we would automatically have diagnosed this right away,' he said, in a rather offhand manner. I refrained from telling him that Peter had been in India in early 1977, with bad headaches, and had been treated repeatedly with antibiotics for sinus infection. The doctor peered at the X-rays and agreed that there had been something like an abscess formation in the frontal area due to the purulent sinus; that there had been a multiple infection, bacterial superimposed upon an underlying tuberculous process ...

There were the usual repetitions of tests with, of course, resistance from Peter. The physician then told us that Peter should be put in an institution. 'There isn't much hope that he will improve very much now,' said he. He mentioned one institution, in Scotland, which might cater for such 'permanently damaged' people as Peter. 'He will be able to do some manual work, I believe they are quite happy there,' he said, consoling us. 'Of course, in India, we do have clinics, but not with that kind of facility.'

Then what happened to adults suffering from the sequelae of tuberculous meningitis in India, I wondered?

89

They were, if possible, put in clinics; if not, kept at home. But so many of them must be those vagrants, half-mad, joining that population of beggars who fill the slums and seep on to the streets, walking unaware of the traffic between the motor cars, walking 'inebriately' as Peter had done...

I looked at Vincent's face. Politely grim. And I too could not bear, at the time, thinking of Peter, handsome, gifted Peter, being 'in an institution'.

'He'll die in an institution,' I said to Vincent when we were outside.

'Yes, he will.'

So it was decided. We'd keep him in the Family. We'd keep him at home, in Bangalore. We would try to do what an institution could not do. We would try to train what remained undamaged in his brain to function. We would try to open new conduits of behaviour among his neurones. Vincent kept on saying: 'After all, the Swiss doctors told us there was hope.' He clung to this, even though perhaps he interpreted 'hope' to mean 'total recovery'.

Michael and Anne took the mission of caring for Peter seriously. 'We'll look after him,' they said. There would be five servants instead of three. Besides the cook, the cleaner-sweeper already working for the household, and the gardener (and an occasional boy to clean, with ash, all the metal plates and utensils), Vincent hired a special servant, an untouchable, to wash Peter's clothes and keep the room clean, since he still dirtied himself frequently. He would now refuse to wear the protective pants. And since there was a servant to do the laundry, we did away with them. He would still leap up from the toilet seat unless held down. A bodyguard, or medical orderly, was also hired. He would come in the morning and stay all day, to watch Peter, to see that he did not run out of the house, to see he did not hurt himself when no one was about. He left in the evening.

I had had previous stays in Bangalore, most pleasant stays, with Vincent and Michael and Anne. But now Peter absorbed all our thoughts, all our energies. Everything we did was geared to Peter. Anne, who had a fixed job, teaching in a school for the mentally handicapped, did not directly participate. But Michael was in and out of the house, and he was the one, therefore, who would be in charge of Peter when Vincent returned with me to Switzerland.

In the evenings we would sit on the verandah, and talk, while Peter paced the garden. He went into periods of frenzied activity, with obsessional movements. Every week the doctor would change the drugs; increase or decrease the dosage, vary the combinations. Rows of pills. Rows of schedules ... we wrote them all down. Rows of little boxes and bottles, with Michael in charge.

And one evening Anne showed me the photograph albums. Peter, dressed as Little Lord Fauntleroy. And then it seemed to me that, somehow, this perfection exacted from him so young had been a major factor in his continuing, for so long, to work, forcing himself, until he collapsed. It was also, perhaps, the anchor of his obstinacy. Why he resisted, fought us, fought the doctors. Peter could not accept that there was something radically wrong with him.

Very soon after reaching Bangalore, Vincent and I began to stir his memory.

'Peter, what was it like in Teheran?'

Peter looked away. 'Iran,' he said, 'Iran ... ' and began to giggle.

'Remember, Peter, you asked me what I thought of the Shah?'

Peter walked away.

'Peter, remember Switzerland? Lausanne? Flims? Remember your searching for your keys in the snow?'

And Peter, unsmiling, said: 'Yes ... the snow, the lake ... '

And so, patchily, painstakingly, Vincent would put him in touch with himself, his own past. Would try to reconstruct for Peter a coherence of the past.

I could not stay for ever; I had to work, to write, to go to China. My own relatives, friends, their children, to care for. It was agreed that I would return first to Switzerland and Vincent would come later, when Peter was quite settled in Bangalore.

I was back for a week when Vincent telephoned to say he would be delaying his return ... though Peter was getting on well.

I should have known.

Suddenly, I saw what would happen. Vincent was dividing himself in two. One part of him would care for Peter, look after Peter, be in India with Peter ...

Another part – that was for me.

I should have known. I would pay for Peter in accepting solitude – aloneness. All the rest, the financial items, the planes, the travel, the extras, were minor factors. Peter's company had paid for the great bulk of the medical expenses.

Vincent would come and go, go and come, between us, between me and Peter

And what else could I do, but accept that, for half of each year, I would be alone? And that, therefore, I must begin to shape my life as if one day, one day, Vincent would not be there. An apprenticeship of solitude was before me – and it would last many years.

I worked; I had much to do; but now I realized that my contribution to Peter would be my own loneliness. My having to do everything, from now on, myself, for myself.

I should have known.

When we decided that Peter would not be institutionalized, it was clear that, although Michael and Anne would look after him, Vincent would have to go back and forth, between me and Peter, between Europe and India, for he would not, I knew, feel at peace with himself otherwise.

What would our life together be like now?

It is hard to describe exactly what I felt. Angry, yes;

feeling unwanted, feeling that Vincent was unfair to me. And saying it to him on the telephone ... and then, immediately afterwards, remorseful, guilty, thinking I was unbearably selfish, and urging Vincent to stay as long as he liked away from me ...

Was I lonely? Yes and no. Lonely because there was no physical presence, no warmth and laughter, because at night I slept badly, alone, in the apartment, waking up at the slightest noise. Not lonely, because I had so much to do, so many friends.

To say that I accepted this situation in silence, with abnegation and gentle, selfless self-effacement would be a lie. I shouted, screamed (mostly within myself). 'I'm your wife! But you treat me like something ... extraneous ... just an interpolation ... it's Peter, Peter, all the time now.'

Vincent has a way of just keeping quiet. But his mind buzzes away, until he finds the thing that will hurt most. 'You don't need me any more ... you're strong, you're successful ... Peter needs me ... '

With little variation, for the next eight years, this would be his excuse, his rampart, his explanation.

'You don't need me ... Peter needs me.'

Until it almost became true. Having to do everything, from filling forms for the post office to keep my mail when I'm away, to coping with bank accounts, with bills, with lawyers; having to endure some very nasty attacks (and the malice, and mendacity, which inspired them) alone, deciding, replying to letters, fashioning my own living without Vincent, it is quite true that now I do not *need* him as a helpmate, a partner, someone on whose shoulder I can weep. He has no comfort to offer me; if I complain of something he will tell me how badly I handled the matter, how *he* would have done it. Only he was simply *not there* to do it.

And that is what Peter has done to me, to us.

I saw it in 1978; but only like a sudden chill – a premonition of disaster.

93

I was writing a book. I fought against apprehension, against jealousy, because I had to protect my book from becoming unfocused. And Vincent was necessary, so necessary, for the end of my book. Not his physical presence, but my sureness that he was not being taken from me.

'You're making up things in your mind. Of course you'll always come first with Vincent – it's you he loves – and if you love him, then you must also love and care for his son, Peter.'

I could not stay in India, in the house in Bangalore. It was not possible for me to write, to work in India. I had tried, several times; but I could not. Too beguiling the climate, too removed also from my preoccupations the culture. Or rather, should I live in India, I would be in perpetual turmoil, because so many things in that society of tremendous inequalities would solicit my involvement ... and not to be involved would be almost impossible for me. And Vincent, too, knew that though I loved him, I could not live in his country. 'You need the air of China at least twice a year, one day you'll go back and settle there, I know,' he had said. Perhaps he would settle in India, with Peter ...

Thus through 1978, 1979 ... to and fro, back and forth. And then in September 1979 Vincent and I went together to China, taking with us Michael and Peter.

VII

Taking Peter to China was an act of faith; also a foolishness; born of that confidence which Vincent exuded, which spilled over on me. For Peter now had bursts of apparent lucidity; his conversations with his father seemed, to the latter, reasonable; to me, they sounded merely imitative, but I was not sure. I think what happened was the following.

Vincent to Peter: 'Peter, I'm going to China with Suyin.'

Peter: 'Daddy, I want to go to China with you.'

Vincent to me: 'Peter would like to go to China.'

Me: 'Well, perhaps it will stimulate him, do him some good...'

I think that is how it happened. Vincent had not been to China since late August 1977, when his trip had been interrupted, at my own urging, after I had heard Peter's voice on the telephone. Even today, I still hear with that memory of sentience beyond words the grinding, pebbly voice, each syllable painfully wrenched out of Peter's larynx by his failing will.

95

It was now two years later; Peter had shown some improvement, though he was still incontinent every two or three days. He was at times hyperactive, at times still had bouts of somnolence. He still had to be told to wake up, to wash himself, to go to bed. But at times he would seem quite clear, and alert. And he could use a slide rule to calculate sums.

Each time I went to China my friends would enquire with affectionate concern about Peter, and Vincent. They gave me much comfort. I was relieved of all worry regarding Vincent and my relationship with him when away from him, in China. It was as if, in China, love took on added amplitude, an exoneration from time and space frameworks, became a totality in which I moved, where physical nearness, proximity, no longer mattered. As real as air and water, fire and earth, was the unseen person; knowledge of his existence satisfaction enough.

Metamorphosis of memory into joy. Sureness that what was will ever be, because nothing could be effaced. I was far more certain of solid, enduring love when away from Vincent in China; and perhaps, for him, it was in India that he loved me most.

Each of us, in our country, within our own web of relationships; not contradicting the couple we are, but reinforcing it. As the spider uses length and breadth of emptiness to shape its web, so perhaps we needed distance and absence as well as presence and proximity. Perhaps that is why I was persuaded that a trip to China might work for Peter the miracle that Vincent expected.

Michael, of course, came with Peter. I thought Michael, for his devoted care of Peter, would feel happy with a trip to China, still difficult to arrange for Indian passport-holders. Anne had to stay with her three sons, and she also had a job she could not leave. I think she was pleased to be relieved of Peter's presence; it was now over a year that it had been impossible for her and her husband to go out together at night; to go to parties, or even to a movie, except when

Vincent was with them. 'I can leave the children with the servant, they'll be all right,' said Anne. 'But we don't know about Peter ... '

Michael's devotion to his brother's welfare was certain; and he cheerfully agreed to come to China. The three of them flew to Beijing together. I had arrived earlier, not only in order to prepare everything, but also to be able to do all I had to do (see friends, give talks, research into conditions in the villages and in the cities under the new reforms, with the policies of opening up precipitating social change as well as economic change) before the three arrived, when I would be busy taking them round sightseeing. My Chinese friends assured me that they were delighted to have Peter as their guest. Doctors would be available if needed. A young interpreter would look after Peter and Michael. China's generosity towards friends is matchless. 'Just tell us what we can do to help and we shall do it,' the Chinese said to me.

The air trip was nightmarish. In Bombay, suddenly, Peter resisted getting on to the plane, and there had been quite a scene at the airport, with Peter finally being pushed into his seat in the Air-India jet to Hong Kong. He was restive throughout the flight, but in Hong Kong seemed calmer. With Vincent and Michael on either side, he walked a little; but all meals were consumed in his room. They arrived in Beijing, my friends and I expectant at the airport. Peter came down, and for a while, as he saw me, appeared 'normal'.

'Hello,' he said.

'Did you have a nice trip?'

'Yes. I'm in China now.'

'Yes, Peter, you are.'

'I don't understand Chinese.'

'But Peter, everyone is speaking English with you ... '

We all arm ourselves with dreams; how otherwise can we keep on living? It is the dreams that die first; and we then carry their corpses about with us, a load we try to forget.

It was a dream – which shattered almost immedi-

97

ately – that Peter, in China, would be 'stimulated', would be 'interested'. The Indian doctors, Vincent, myself, we were trying to arouse his brain, to establish new connections – and so far there had been progress, in that Peter *recognized* situations, was aware of the content of our talk. He seemed happy to see me at the airport, I was a *point de repère*, an anchor, to him; almost he believed he was back in Paris, he shone, sweatily, saying drunkenly: 'Oh, you know, I want to tell you ... ' but he never ended his sentence. I knew what he wanted to tell me. That he loved me. That his love for me was muddled but a most vivid thing for him; that he felt both elated and ashamed, and so never finished his sentences.

But now it was different. Neither Vincent nor I could do anything except watch, horrified, Peter going berserk in China. Watch his panic. In our suite at the hotel he paced, paced, frantically, to the telephone and back ...

'Ring Air-India, get me a plane, I can't stay here ... '

'But, Peter, you said you wanted to come.'

'Ring the airport. I want to go away.'

I had never believed in culture shock, having myself never experienced it. I knew, though, that the mere sight of a physical configuration different from the usual one, the sound of a different language, can awaken in some people an abysmal, uncontrollable terror.

Culture shock. Peter now exhibited a bad case of it, throughout the eight days he was in Beijing; eight days only, instead of the planned sixteen. I knew only of one other instance almost as bad. The children of some Indian friends of ours, both born in Switzerland, when taken home to India by their parents, went into frenzied terror in Bombay because, for them, there were just too many people on the streets ... they refused to come out of their rooms, and had to be taken back to Switzerland.

Peter could not be taken anywhere. He paced and paced the hotel floor, and the thick pink carpet of his room and of our suite began to slough wads of pink wool. Where, in the brain, does this reaction to body difference, sound difference, reside? Is it not the essential basis of racism? Something usually ignored but, suddenly, wreaking havoc, finding its own unreasonable reasons, a volcanic eruption, unamenable to explanation ... Why did Peter react as he did?

From Peter's staggering frenzy I thought I could, perhaps, understand what I had never understood: culture shock. Surely a euphemism for something more archetypal, coming from the buried millennia of man's stage on earth ...

Peter and Michael shared a room on the same floor of the hotel as our suite. All meals had to be taken to Peter's room as he refused to go down to the restaurant. He pretended not to see the amiable, helpful waiters who, once they knew that he was ill, learnt to say: 'Peter, how are you?' and deployed prodigious eagerness to help. He was not actually violent, but on the third day began to get attacks of diarrhoea, which were actually his way of 'expelling' what he hated (for it would recur, on other occasions). Vincent and Michael spent a great deal of time cleaning the room and bathroom floors. We could not ask the hotel staff to do this. Every time Peter saw me he would say: 'Please, please ring up the airline ... ask the plane to take me to Bangalore.' By the fourth day we realized that we must indeed get a plane for him. He could not stay.

On the sixth day we had one booked for two days later. We told Peter and he appeared to calm down. I suggested that perhaps he would like to see a doctor.

'Yes, I'm not well, but I won't understand his Chinese.'

'He'll talk to you in English.'

'No, he can't, he's Chinese.'

We went to the hospital, but as soon as Peter was in the consulting room with Dr Zhang he went into another crisis, trying to rush out, screaming, refusing any examination. He rolled his eyes, and shook all over, convulsively.

'I'm afraid he must have some schizophrenic tendencies.

They probably antedate his meningitis,' said the baffled Dr Zhang, who had seen thousands of patients with sequelae of meningitis, but none quite like Peter.

I could not say to Dr Zhang: 'No, he's merely exhibiting an extreme form of culture shock.'

Peter was in such a state of agitation that (with enormous difficulty) a calming injection was given to him. In the car he got a massive bout of diarrhoea and we apologized to the driver, who had to clean it up. Vincent and Michael cleaned Peter once we had re-entered the hotel room.

The only two times in those eight days when, extraordinarily enough, Peter behaved well was when I asked a Eurasian friend of mine, living in China, to get her nephew to look after Peter while we were attending a dinner given for us by Madame Deng Yingchao, the widow of the late Prime Minister Zhou Enlai. And another time when, for a few hours, I took Michael out to see the Imperial Palaces and the Square of Heavenly Peace in front of the Forbidden City. My friend Hualan (Polish mother, Chinese father, herself conversant in nine languages) brought her nephew, Alex. His father was Russian, his mother was Hualan's sister. Hence, in the crossing of the genes, Alex was born with blue eyes and fairish hair. Which, since he was a Chinese citizen, educated and brought up in China, made life a puzzle for him at times. He was constantly being treated as a foreigner in his own land; given privileges (people making way for him at the post office, in buses), but at other times restrained, when he wanted to attend meetings, by guards who did not know that he was really Chinese. He had been of the age to be sent to the countryside, as a Red Guard during the Cultural Revolution, and this had interfered with his ambition to become an engineer. Now he was back at the university, studying, but did not feel entirely at ease because he was still the 'foreigner', due to his physical appearance.

This does happen to Eurasians, and it marks them. I felt lucky, in that my looks are more or less nondescript: dark hair, Chinese eyes, Chinese body build; but definitely something un-Chinese too, so that in China I am often asked whether I come from Sinkiang, that outward western province of China which has five million Uighurs, or Central Asians, whose looks are often a cross between the West and the Mongol races. But more important than looks is body language; a satisfyingly descriptive phrase from America, which despite being so racially heterogeneous, still conveys an American flavour through gestures, tones, behaviour, among its so diverse peoples; and so all my life I have mimicked 'body language', according to where I am. Thus in France I can behave in a French way; in China in a Chinese way. It is this physical 'gesture pattern' which really impinges upon the unconscious, and defines the person, as it also defines a class, a caste.

Peter reacted well to Alex. Because, to him, Alex looked *familiar*. He looked like the Belgians Peter had worked with. And then I began to understand also why, in India, the caste feeling is still so strong. Why even such an Indian as Ved Mehta, acclaimed in America, could say to someone who commented on his skin colour that he was not black, but Aryan, and quite unlike 'the Dravidians' of India. Now Vincent and his family are Dravidians, and keenly conscious at times of the colour feeling in their own country. Racism, then, appeared to me part of what is called 'culture shock', or perhaps its fundamental reason...or rather unreason. Built-in racism, in body cell and bone, totally irrational, just beneath the skin, and so enormously dangerous.

On the fifth day, I noticed that Peter's ankle was bleeding.

'Did you hurt yourself, Peter?'

'No...I want a plane, get me a plane to Bangalore...'

Had he accidentally bumped against something? While I peered at his ankle he said, dully: 'Michael kicked me because I'm a naughty boy.'

Michael. I confronted him. 'Michael, did you hit Peter?'

101

'Yes, I did. I'm sorry, but he really at times cannot be controlled. He listens to Daddy, not to me. I had to prevent him from shitting right in the middle of the room. I had to kick his ankle to stop him.'

And then Michael and I had a long talk. He poured out his grievances. Michael was now convinced that, in his father's eyes, he was merely useful as his brother's keeper, merely being used, conveniently. There were also, perhaps, childhood memories, sibling resentments there; Peter being his mother's favourite. Yet Michael had great qualities, great potential; he was a man of strong emotions, and very well-educated. He read enormously, and remembered what he read. It was, of course, not pleasant for him to have to spend many hours a day chaperoning Peter, in and out of the hotel (mostly in). And Michael still had to spend every night in the room, in the bed next to Peter's.

'What kind of a holiday am I getting in China? I've only been asked to come to wash up Peter's shit,' said Michael.

I took Michael out for a walk while Vincent stayed with Peter. In any family there is the fact that, of all the people we know, it is our siblings who are unchosen. A brother, a sister, is always something not altogether welcome; often resented, but to be lived with, to be tolerated. How do we achieve love, affection, solidarity with siblings when the Cain and Abel situation is the main factor in brother-to-brother relations, recognized – oh, with such talent – in the Bible, before psychologists and psychiatrists were invented? Sisterly resentment, mother–daughter repulsion, exists strongly, in all societies, under all cultures. The Greeks, those geniuses of the mind and heart, showed it openly in their tragedies, consecrated these impulses in their gods. Why close our minds to all this? But, in the end, compromise, co-living, a necessary apparatus of lies and the balm of outward expressions (routine) of love is what most of us (myself included) must achieve to go on living and, in the end, to go on really caring, for we are all so many-layered, so contradictory, in that part of the brain which scientists tell us is still our undeveloped, primal self.

Michael was both devoted to his brother, and to his father, and a bit resentful. Because Peter, once his mother's favourite, was now absorbing all his father's attention. I not only sympathized, I felt, at times, exactly as he did. Michael is fundamentally capable of great loyalty, of giving and also of self-sacrifice. Without really knowing it, Vincent was ordering Michael about. Do this. Do that. Peter wants. Peter must have.

Hence I not only do not blame Michael, I myself – because I must tell the truth – have hit Peter. Just a slap on the shoulder, pounding his arm, but all of them active physical gestures of resentment. He takes it as play; he provokes me as much as he can so that I shall do this. Only once, when I hit a little bit harder (usually my 'hitting' is symbolic, a slap which can even be translated as affectionate), he said, wonderingly: 'Oh, that hurt.' And smiled, with great satisfaction, as at something accomplished.

Michael truly loved his father; felt his love unrequired in some respects. Anne had told me: 'He tries to be like his father in so many ways. He collects everything about his father ... ' I think she was a little jealous; Michael was only exhibiting the pattern of the Family, close-knit, close-found, almost, at times, impermeable to 'the others', the in-laws whom Patricia wittily called 'outlaws'.

'Anne, this is an Indian family. You'll find Jewish families are like that. And Chinese families too.'

'I think Peter's just pretending,' Michael said. 'He's always much worse when Daddy's around.'

'Why don't you have a good talk with your father, bring him to discuss it with you, and tell him how you feel?'

It was partly true that Vincent exhibited a certain difference in attitude towards his eldest son, perhaps because he expected his eldest son to *do* so much more (again so typical: in Chinese families very often the eldest son sweats away all his life to furnish the money to send his siblings to school, to university). This difference was imperceptible, except in tone of voice, a certain behaviour. Actually, Vincent was treating Michael as an adult, and Peter and Patricia still as children, but this realization had not come to Michael. There are so many nuances in a family. I was sensitive to them, having to cope with a Chinese family as well as an Indian one, and also beginning to grasp the intricacies of an American family relationship (which is based, very often, on an avoidance of relationship in the name of independence). I was sensitive to the fact that, when speaking to Michael, his father would at times look away as if he was addressing the air. This was because Vincent felt so sure that Michael would understand, and he was merely thinking aloud in front of him. But words, and attitudes adopted when words are spoken, shape meanings and deform them. Sometimes a syllable more or less will convey, in that emotional soup which is a family – every family – a feeling of rejection. There was, as Michael saw it, something missing in his dialogue with his father. How eagerly he had agreed to look after Peter. But his father was still running the show.

'I've been more than fair to all my children,' was Vincent's reply when I started talking about the situation (and why should I be so concerned about his children, except that, fundamentally, I am a person who forever gets involved). Indeed he had been fair, but the word 'fair' meant, to him, according to needs. Peter needed him most at the moment; as Patricia had needed him, some years back. Now she no longer needed him. She was married, and happy; but Peter needed him. And because of this, he was even sacrificing me, in a way ...

I made a mistake now. I thought that the father-son relationship gone slightly awry could be worked out through talk. 'You must stand up to your father and tell him how you feel. I've always stood up to him and discussed everything, and it's worked out fine. He is accessible to reason, you know.' I explained that throughout life, with our brothers and sisters and our parents, we go through a process of having constantly to readjust ourselves, constantly redefine the territorial limits of our personality, and their encroachments on us. The human being is not static; it is in a state of flux, an ever-changing star; and once we know this, we know that every day, every hour, we have to be on the lookout for change. 'But it's important to keep relationships going,' I said. 'They root us; we need them, like plants need fertilizers. To abscond, to flee from them, is failure. It's a rubbing-out of ourselves when we rub out others. Traumatic, in the end self-defeating.' I thought back to my own childhood; wreckage which might have swamped me, conquered by not giving up; and now, with my own siblings, I had achieved marvellous new links, a redefinition of our mutual roles, based on the roles we had assumed towards each other when we were children, but now aggrandized, understood.

'You cannot expect your father to understand you unless you explain to him how you feel, Michael.'

Michael nodded, the Indian way, that way of nodding which still baffles me, after thirty years with an Indian. Then Vincent and Michael and Peter left, returning to India. I remained in China for a while. After all, China was my root, my life-sustaining source, and here there was so much to do, another life, many other lives to care for, an enormous Big Family, and I was part of it, totally involved – yet at the same time, I was also part of the world outside China; part of the Western world, and now, because of Vincent, part of India. I had to live up to all those roles; to all that life demanded of me. Karma.

Four weeks later I returned to India, to find that Peter was in hospital for a readjustment of his drugs and a check-up. Temporarily we were free of him, of his impact upon Michael and Anne, of the constant strain he imposed upon his father. Anne had always suffered from migraine headaches, and they had been getting more frequent in the last year.

VIII

Anne, in shopping excursions with me, told me more about herself than she did while in the house. Reticence, good breeding, made her preserve a polished amiability, underlaid by a nervous fear of not being considered good-mannered enough, when at home. But outside, going from shop to shop, she unwrapped herself of her Anglo-Indian inhibitions and I discovered that she had both spirit and ambition. She wanted to continue studying. Marriage, and three children, had come too early for her. She worked hard and well at the school for the mentally handicapped, and would win a prize for her work. But now she wanted to go back to university, to get a degree.

'I want to make something of myself before it is too late. The day will come when my three children won't need me. I want to be something before I'm too old.' The strong resolve in slight, childish-looking Anne reminded me of my adolescent self. She came from a family where there had been much outward expression of love and concern, perhaps because such extrovert exhibition of affection is reassurance, and Heaven knows the in-between people, Eurasians, Anglo-Indians, need reassurance. Now she was an in-law in an Indian family with totally Indian behaviour, which is restrained, as is Chinese behaviour. 'It is typical of the Family never to show affection,' said Anne, somewhat bitterly. I had to agree that the Family is rather inarticulate in words, in gestures such as touching, fondling. But Anne mistook this for coldness, whereas it was only that total internalization of emotion (already present in Appa) which was also present in Patricia, in Peter, in Michael, in their father ... and was also there in my Chinese family, which of course thinks exuberance total bad manners. No *gesture*, hand or arm around one's shoulder, or kissing, in times of distress. Only the eyes, the eyes, the look, full of all that is unspoken, undemonstrated. I had been trained to all this; I knew that lack of expression of concern does not mean coldness. But I understood Anne. 'Most people in Asia do not show their emotions, Anne. That doesn't mean they haven't got feelings. Vincent is a very affectionate and kind person, but he won't hold my hand in public, he'd think it indecent.'

Anne sighed. She was a bit Western in her need for patting, touching, being made to feel wanted and precious. I told her about my attempt, while in Paris, to walk arm-in-arm with Vincent, and his astonishment. In India, of course, this was not done, not at all, oh no, no, and it was only beginning in China...

Peter's presence, the constant strain it imposed upon both Michael and Anne, had begun to affect Michael's temper. Michael had never been a patient man, and now there would be trivia, small things cropping up, where Vincent the Father would make the decisions, and not expect anything but acquiescence, no demur, no discussion. Because this was the pattern. Dominant male. And Michael felt it; Anne felt it. It grated upon Anne, because in a way she felt the Bangalore house was *her* home; she lived in it, took care of it. It was her envelope, part of her personality.

She had a wonderful way with flowers and plants, and had made the garden quite delightful with the help of an old *mali*, or gardener. When Vincent took away the hand-embroidered doilies she lovingly placed under every statuette, every cup, every vase, Anne would get a migraine. She was prone to migraines. She would retire, mute, to bed. I told Vincent: 'You're lucky to have a woman like me around, who doesn't put doilies everywhere, and doesn't care about stitching, embroidering, or knitting.' All activities which Vincent hates.

On his return from China Peter had spent three weeks in hospital, both for his recurring bouts of diarrhoea and for extreme, uncontrollable agitation. Peter had had, of course, amoebic dysentery (I think fully three-fifths of the Indian population have had amoebic infection), and everyone wondered whether he had had a recurrence, or whether it was 'psychosomatic diarrhoea'. As he quietened down with tranquillizers, so did his intestinal perturbation, and Vincent, who had stayed on to watch over his son, now returned home, and we would phone every Sunday from Lausanne to Bangalore, to enquire how Peter was. I think this also exacerbated the friction that was beginning between himself and the young couple. They felt they were not entirely trusted. Vincent now received letters from Michael which I was not shown, but which seemed to disturb him, though the general tenor was that all was well with Peter. I know when something worries Vincent. He grows more silent, and I knew he was planning to fly back to India because he was worried. I felt that his going would not do any good, and anyway I too was exasperated. 'You're married to me, not to Peter, I only see you about six to seven months a year. You're planning to spend next Christmas and New Year with Peter, not with me. Not that I care about Christmas, New Year, or even my birthday, when very often you're not there. Or about anniversaries for our marriage, which you always forget anyway. But have you asked yourself, ever, how I feel about all this?'

Poor darling. My poor darling husband. He said, feebly: 'You don't need me as much as Peter does. You've got China, a whole world of your own; you've got your books...' This would be his recurring theme, for all the years of Peter's illness, and of course he was right. He was right because it is true that, in a way, I've got so much more of the world and its marvels to become involved in. But he has that internal universe of emotion, without which I desiccate. He never hesitated to give up whatever is known as success, achievement, because I was more important to him than his own success. But now what he meant was: 'You are the strong one. You will survive and achieve. Even without me. But Peter needs me, needs me, and I must go where I am needed.' And of course he was right. I am strong, healthy – I too must contribute to Peter's recall from sickness to health, from abnormality to semi-normality... whatever the word normality means. This has nothing to do with that rapacious world we live in, in which we tread upon the weak ones. This is a universe of caring and sharing... even if it is hard to live up to it all the time.

Michael was also caught within the torment both of achieving himself and of achieving self-abnegation. Abnegation which impinged upon and flawed, perhaps, his perception of his own role in caring for his young brother. He, and even more so Anne, felt themselves perfectly capable of dealing with Peter. Michael truly wanted to make a success out of looking after Peter; he did not want, all the time, his father checking, telling him what to do or not to do. I was much aware of this, but it was very difficult to intervene, and I was also a little worried about the way Michael envisaged his duty. Michael and Anne, in some ways, were too scientifically-minded; and the words 'It is better to be strict with Peter' recurred in some of Michael's letters. Obviously, the notion that Peter was faking, was 'putting on a show', had not left him; and at times I too felt that Peter was deliberately trying to get us all angry with him.

109

Michael felt that Peter needed discipline; he believed sincerely in an orderly style of life for Peter. And Vincent seemed to overrule this; allowing Peter to turn up late for meals; perhaps to sleep late in the morning...

I thought Vincent's way was, on the whole, the best for Peter. He was inculcating in him a return to physical habits of cleanliness, manners at table, but in other ways gave him much latitude; allowing him to *say* all he wanted; and even to wander about (always attended, of course), while everyone waited for him to turn up. He wanted Peter to feel more or less unrestricted, even with a bodyguard about all the time. He would encourage Peter to go to see his friends. Peter would go, visit them in their houses, with the bodyguard waiting outside. Vincent even suggested, and Anne would give, parties, where a boisterous Peter was the host, in the house. As much as possible, Vincent exposed Peter to a normal life, to other people. And the fact that Peter remembered his old life, remembered his friends' names, and would be almost uncontrollably happy to see them, seemed to Vincent encouraging signs of recovery.

Michael's ideas were somewhat different. And they became even more distant from Vincent's when Anne and he became acquainted with a certain visiting Western professor, a psychologist, whom they now consulted on the subject of Peter. It seems the psychologist was convincing them of the need for 'discipline', and after that I heard nothing else but 'how to deal with Peter' formulas, culled straight from this psychologist's jargon. I do not know whether the expert (who, surely, had great qualifications and merit) understood Peter's problem, or had any real experience of the devious, wayward, protean, unpredictable manifestations that arise from sequelae of tuberculous meningitis.

Peter would be walking along the road. He would stop, stare at someone, go up to him and ask: 'What do you think of India?' or 'Do you believe in God?' Surprised, apprehensive, courteous, the man addressed would glance at the

bodyguard, or at Vincent, and then answer, good-
naturedly, or merely smile and walk away. Peter would see
a beggar on the street and go up to him and give him
money. Vincent allowed him pocket money, to boost
Peter's faith in himself. For many, many months, Peter
would give away all the money on him, give and give. And
Vincent let him do so. Peter would talk to all the tri-motor
wallahs who puff away at frenzied speeds, weaving their
small yellow buglike vehicles in the surging traffic. He
would ask them what they thought of the caste system, and
how much they earned a day. One of them became his
friend, and even wrote a card to him: 'Peter, you are my
frend.'

We had, in that year of 1980, also taken Peter to
restaurants, where he shouted and waved his arms about, so
that we had to take him back. But the waiters smiled. They
understood. Vincent persisted. 'We've got to keep on
trying ... if he's kept away from everything, he'll never
learn ... ' Vincent's idea to 'stimulate' Peter in every way, to
interest him, applied also to me. I was a great 'stimulator'
for Peter. 'He loves talking to you,' Vincent said. I do not
know whether the word 'talking' was quite right, but I
tried.

But Michael's psychologist felt that people who are not
normal must be kept under strict 'control', and must be
protected. Protection, in a sense, really meant being restricted, almost isolated. This is done by many families, who are
ashamed to be seen with their abnormal children, and keep
them closeted, or put them away, or simply cannot cope
with all that has to be done, with the responsibility, the
unrelenting demand for attention. Hence the use of
tranquillizers, to keep them torpid, lethargic. Vincent's
ideas to utilize all of us to 'awaken' whatever cells Peter's
brain could muster, to create, or re-create, new responses
and behaviour, was not a very easy experiment to carry
through.

In that year I was subject to much stress; once I became ill

111

with flu and remember one morning alone in Lausanne, when dizzy with fever I could ring up no one (it was Sunday morning) except my friends at the Chinese embassy in Geneva. Of course they came, immediately, with antibiotics and solicitude. But I felt bitter, deprived, also ashamed. I did not want at the time to be the object of any pity. Once again jealousy came, jeering at me. I didn't count. What was I, what was happening to the couple we were, in this situation? Why should I be thus utilized? Why should I accept all this ... I felt very sorry for myself, and it lasted a good two days.

Vincent returned, announcing that everything had been fixed after a talk with Michael. 'I've told him what to do,' said Vincent.

'I missed you,' I said.

'I missed you too,' he replied, meaning it.

'Then I'll tell you that you haven't really fixed anything. Michael is not happy with the way things are. I think you should arrange to have Peter six months with your brothers and sisters in Madras and six months with Michael in Bangalore. In this way, the strain won't be so intense on Michael and Anne.'

'I asked Peter and he doesn't want to leave Bangalore,' said Vincent, ingenuously.

'He'll say and do anything to remain a baby. He wants to be a baby. He told me: "I want to be a baaaaby." Right now he's on a regression pattern.'

'How do you know?'

'I feel it.'

Of course Vincent did not believe me. 'We'll see.'

A few more weeks. Vincent's brother Basil went to Bangalore, and wrote a guarded, cautious letter. I could imagine what was happening. Peter, who enjoyed at times going for walks (with Vincent and the bodyguard) to the market streets, would help himself to a dish, or a drink, and then walk off, while the bodyguard paid up. But now the walks were curbed, because he did not behave well.

Michael faithfully took him to the doctor and to the psychologist, and reported that they approved of the new regime. He wrote:

> Peter's mental recovery has not been encouraging. This may be attributed to the following: his emotional background during his childhood with its unfortunate molly-coddling which has left him an emotional cripple ... his lack of ability to make a policy decision.

I read the words. Where had Michael learnt this jargon? Obviously from the psychologist.

> We must stop handling him with kid gloves. His medical orderly [the bodyguard] is superfluous. His diet must be strictly controlled and frugal ... his meals must be used as a reward for completing tasks.

Oh damn, damn; what tasks could Peter perform? And who would urge him to do them, keeping his concentration on what he was doing? The whole approach was 'scientific', but it would not work for Peter.

Anne also wrote, totally approving of Michael's plan to turn Peter into a well-behaved, hard-working, normal human being ... when I read these letters, I knew something was going to explode. And I realized better what Vincent was trying to do; and how difficult it was. But Vincent was right. He knew his son, knew his obstinacy. Knew that Peter could never be forced or driven.

I thought again of Vincent, of his kindness, of the way in which if anyone said to him: 'Will you help me?' he reacted immediately, willingly. Peter was also like that. He had to be coaxed, appealed to. He could not be forced. Peter had wanted to be a priest. He had refused an excellent job in order to dig wells in villages.

I now remembered one occasion when Vincent was in India, and I had raged at him on the telephone. 'I've been ill,' I had shouted. 'I can't go on like this.'

'Then I'll come back right away,' Vincent had said. And I was ashamed.

'No, don't. I'm just making it up. I'm not ill, just a little fed up.'

'But what can I do?' Vincent's voice said on the telephone.

'Just what you're doing, I suppose.' All the things Vincent used to do to help me ... but now he had another priority. 'Vincent, you must go back to India. Peter's not going to do well in Bangalore. You must take him to Madras.'

So back again to India, Vincent first, and me a little later, flying alone and landing in Bombay. Bombay airport is a great test of patience to any traveller. The procedures are most cumbersome. This is not the fault of the Indian customs officers, or the clerks who meticulously check the passports, stamp, restamp, fill a form, enter something in a book, then pass on the whole thing, passport and forms included, to another official who counterchecks ... and all this happens usually between 2 a.m. and 7 a.m., when the planes come in from Europe, from the Gulf States. There are always long, long queues, always being added to as plane after plane disgorges passengers. For Bombay is a busy airport, and there is also a lot of smuggling through the city: not only drugs, but gold, and jewellery, so the customs officers check the luggage (and there is usually an immense amount of luggage, chiefly from the Arab and Indian travellers who land here) very thoroughly. Almost every day the Indian press publishes, triumphantly, how gold, or drugs, was discovered 'concealed in a radio' or 'stowed into a mattress'.

At one time there were obliging porters, who for five rupees would carry one's luggage out of the airport. But now there are trolleys, and it makes getting out of the airport even more traumatic, ego-shredding. It is impossible for a woman alone to get a trolley, because these are kept outside the airport and seldom wheeled in. Indian gentlemen, leaving wife and children in charge of the luggage (an average of ten suitcases for a family of four) masterfully stride out of the airport, assault in gentlemanly fashion other Indian males similarly engaged in looking for a trolley, and return triumphantly, sometimes with two or three trolleys ... but a woman alone is handicapped. I've carried my two suitcases, a shoulder bag and a handbag, clutching my passport and customs form (sometimes between my teeth) to walk through the narrow exit always blocked by forceful gentlemen pushing trolleys in, or out, to find Vincent anxiously, patiently waiting down the exit corridor for me. 'Couldn't you get a trolley?' he asks. I feel like exploding. But I don't.

This time, I noticed that Vincent looked worried. 'Peter's not too well. He's got diarrhoea and he's thin ... I think he gets on Michael's nerves.'

We went to Bangalore the next afternoon and Michael greeted me with a good, hearty smile. Dear, anxious, well-meaning Michael, trying so hard to do what was right. Perhaps he felt that I was a little his accomplice, because I had told him in China: 'You'd better talk it out with your father.'

Peter was in his room. 'He's asleep,' said Michael. I waited, and then Peter rose as it was now tea time, and indeed I was a little shocked. He was extremely thin. He had lost at least ten pounds in weight. He was, however, as usual excited and boisterous and screaming and waving his hands about when he saw me. 'You know, I like you very very much ... you know, I can't tell you ... ' Abruptly he got up, walked out, then walked back to me. 'Tell me, do you believe in God?'

'No, Peter.'

'But that's a mortal sin ... '

'Too bad.'

He laughed, giggled, then a spasm seized him and his foot

began to move, helplessly tapping the floor.

'Calm down, calm down,' Vincent said to him.

'Yes, Daddy.' He calmed down. 'I want to tell you, you know, I'm not well.'

Vincent had tried to tell Michael that he felt the psychologist was wrong. Michael was aggrieved. 'Peter keeps on pretending,' he said to me. 'Anne and I have consulted the best psychologist in Bangalore.'

I took Anne for a stroll, to the Bangalore Fine Arts and Crafts building. Among the carved elephants and the inlaid tables I said: 'Anne, Peter is getting too thin ... much too thin ... the treatment may be wrong for him.'

Anne was a bit defensive. 'Yes, he is a bit thin, but the doctor says there's nothing wrong.' But she did acknowledge that, if Peter did not turn up in time for meals, then he did not get anything to eat. 'He's got to learn to eat when everyone else does; otherwise it upsets the children.'

There was nothing wrong; except that Peter was unhappy, Peter was obstinate, and Peter would not eat. I believe that he was also deliberately soiling himself, because he was unhappy, That streak of 'negativeness' in him was coming back; or, rather, he had gone back into it.

That was when the decision was made by Vincent that, for everyone's sake, it would indeed be better for Peter to be half the year in Madras, and half the year in Bangalore with Michael. 'That will diminish the strain on everyone. There's a lot of strain around.'

Except diminish the strain on me, I thought bitterly. But I'm tough, oh yes, tough, and strong, shockingly healthy, there's never anything wrong with me. But seeing Peter's reaction to a well-meaning, but ill-adapted programme, I felt a strong surge of compassion for him, for Vincent, for Michael and Anne. In the end, it was not I, but Vincent who was carrying the heaviest burden of anxiety, and love; who was parcelling himself out between us, who had to make the decisions ...

Vincent took his son to Madras and there he stayed with Aggie, Vincent's youngest sister, her husband Patrick, and their three children. The five lived in that small apartment in the Middle Income Group Housing complex of Foreshore Estate, to which I had been many times since Appa had also stayed there after he left the larger house opposite the cathedral. Peter now had the room which Appa had occupied, and his bathroom too; the three children and their parents managed with another bathroom and one and a half rooms; the half being part of the hallway where the two girls slept at night. It was a very tight fit, and I often wondered how, in the heat of Madras, Patrick and Aggie and their children could endure the discomfort.

'It's quite okay, we'll manage very well,' Patrick said with a broad smile and that sideways Indian shake of the head which means fine, fine. 'Don't worry, Suyin, we'll make Peter comfortable.'

Thomas slept in his parents' room. He was already unable to walk, his leg muscles were wasting, but he could still sit up, and use his arms. He went to school; his mother Aggie taking him with her in a bicycle trishaw every morning and fetching him back. He was very bright, and everyone at school loved him; he got very high marks. In the evening he would sit at table with his parents and sisters, and after that would draw, or write. Later, when a television set was purchased, he would be propped up in his chair in front of the television set and he would watch the programmes, especially the cricket.

The Family now swung into action round Peter. Vincent drew up the schedules for each of them. All in turn would look after Peter. Brother Basil, and Brother Benny, would come, each a day or two a week, to be with Peter. No more orderly. Only Family. Sister Theresa would also come, and Cissy as well. They would have Peter to lunch, regularly, once a week, perhaps more. Theresa would also take Peter for walks in the morning. Later on, when Peter's mother came to stay with Theresa, Peter would go to see his mother, but as she was rather upset by his condition, especially when he shouted, these visits were limited.

Would it be possible for Peter to get used to the cramped conditions?

'I don't like Madras. I want to go back to Bangalore, Daddy.'

'You'll go to Bangalore soon, but at the moment Michael and Anne must have some rest. They got very tired, looking after you.'

'Why, why, that's because I'm crazy, isn't it?'

'No, Peter, you're not crazy. But you've been ill, now you have to pull yourself together, you're already half-way to being well again, soon, soon, you'll be all right...'

'What happened to me, Daddy, tell me, what's really happened to me?'

Peter was conscious that 'something was wrong' with him. At times he would start weeping, knowing that he was 'wrong somewhere'. He would then go to his father, beg him to explain to him why this had taken place. And Vincent explained, and I too at times explained. Yes, he had been ill; it was a germ; no, it had nothing to do with sinning, and he was better, was better. 'Just one more year, son, just one more year... you must write letters, Peter, you've begun writing well again, and you must read, read books.'

'Yes, Daddy.'

Without any theories, without any psychological training, but with sublime and tranquil affection (that sublime tranquillity which came from within their own nature, which had made them accept the verdict on their son, Thomas), Patrick and Aggie, and the rest of the Family, began their routine of caring for Peter. 'Don't worry, we'll take care. Peter needs to feel loved. That's all.'

Michael felt angry. He felt that taking Peter away from Bangalore showed lack of trust in him. It was difficult to explain that it was better for everyone, and chiefly for himself. Peter had been a great strain upon his marriage. In the end, Michael did get over his initial feelings. And

Vincent told me: 'Michael had Peter at the worst time. He tried to do his best.' But it was felt that Peter should not return to Bangalore until he was really stabilized, which did not occur for another three years.

IX

Words are like Japanese screens; curtains behind which people conceal themselves; which prying onlookers lift slightly to glimpse the speaker, the person or object half-revealed. The word is half the sayer, half the one who listens, said Montaigne. For always, between Word and Reality, comes the helplessness of imperfection, the obfuscation embedded in the word, in the thousand unconscious mind taboos, the silencing agent, which makes us prevaricate or euphemize. Where would we be, how could we really live, without some measure of concealment? How can we really face ourselves without going (partly) schizophrenic? And so, revealing Peter, I only reveal what happened to all of us, because of Peter. Peter himself remains *indemne*, untouchable in his world where controls are feeble or lacking. He cannot be ambushed into total discovery.

However, the aim of making Peter better has been successful. This success is due to the Family; to Vincent who never gave up, never faltered in his determination. To

Aggie, Vincent's youngest sister, and her husband Patrick, who from 1980 till the present day never in any way failed to care for Peter in every possible respect. To Basil and Benny and Theresa, Vincent's brothers and sister, who in turn took Peter out, gave him his pills, sat and talked with him, rode buses with him, took trains with him ...

In his first two months in Madras, September to November 1980, Peter put on weight again. His diarrhoea became controlled. Slowly, he became aware of his intestinal functions, and went to the toilet himself. He dirtied himself only once a week, once a fortnight, later once a month ... now, Peter goes for long periods without having an 'accident', as Patrick calls it. He bathes, shaves, dresses himself. He is very careful about his shoes. Vincent buys him smart, Bally Swiss shoes, because Peter likes to be well shod. Peter's need to look well dressed, neat, is an achievement. Of course he has lapses; he has shouting fits, what Patrick and Aggie call 'his not so good days'. But they are getting less as time goes on, and he is never violent, even if at times agitated, extremely so.

Because of Peter, Patrick's apartment has a telephone. As I have already mentioned, telephones in India are very hard to come by (except if one is a big businessman, or a government top official). Appa had one, being a member of the Rajya Sabah. It was promptly removed at his death in 1977. Vincent then went on a spree of calling on bureaucrats with medical certificates, using his connections, to certify that Peter needed a telephone for medical reasons. The telephone was restored. Indian bureaucracy is, like all Asian bureaucracies, only pliable when clout is exhibited. Vincent is good at knowing how to deal with it. Patrick is too timid; Basil and Benny do not have clout. I look at my husband admiringly as he talks, wangles, drives, pushes, and gets his way ...

Also, an air conditioner. This is a great luxury for the Middle Income Group in Madras. Vincent had it installed in Peter's room so that he will feel comfortable in the humid, unrelenting heat of Madras, and sleep well at night. I often think of the others, who swelter ... but do not complain. Not a word of complaint in the last five years from Patrick, Aggie, and their three children, who do not have an air conditioner ...

Surrounded by love, care, affection, patience, unending patience, Peter recouped physically in about two months, and mentally began his long journey to what he is today.

The first sign of progress: he began to read. He read sketchily at first, his attention span, his concentration, not lasting more than three minutes at a time, but since early 1985 it has increased. He did plough through my books. I have found one of them, annotated by him. In the margin he wrote what he thought. It may take him months to get through a book, but he remembers what he reads.

He began to sing. One night we were all together (I was back once again in India, taking time off, between two books, between other pursuits), and Peter began to play the mouth-organ and to sing.

Slow, oh, so plodding, in such zigzag fashion, Peter's crawl back, Peter's brain striving, striving to function ...

His mouth-organ. He had not touched it for years though he had carried it with him to England, to Belgium, to Libya, to Iran. That night he played it, and sang:

> In the *sudden* part of Texas, in the town of
> *Xanafu*
> *Lies* a fortress all in ruins that the weeds
> have overgrown;
> You may look in vain for crosses and you'll
> never see a one,
> But sometimes between the setting and the
> rising of the sun
> You may hear the ghostly bugle as the *troops* go
> marching by
> You can hear them as they answer to that roll
> call in the sky ...

Later, he would write it down, putting *sudden* for southern, *Xanafu* for San Anton, *Lies* for There's, and *troops* for men.

'Peter, Peter, where did you learn that song?'

Peter looks at me, first dully, then trying, groping into his mind, pushing it for recollection.

'I heard it on the radio ... '

'Where?'

Groping again. Trying very hard. It takes about ten minutes. He paces up and down, goes to his room. Returns.

'Where, Peter?'

'In Bangalore ... when I was with Michael and Anne.'

Despite the fact that, physically, Peter had not reacted well in Bangalore, and literally began to starve himself with that particular obstinacy of his, because he did not like discipline, his mind had not been inactive. He would tell his father: 'Michael was right. I was a bad boy, Daddy. I dirtied myself.' He would write to his brother:

> Thank you for your visit ... I hope to be seeing all of you ... I will close with as many 'I like you' as I can manage.

Peter began to write letters. In fact, he had begun writing in Bangalore, before leaving for Madras. This is what he wrote in the summer of 1980:

> My dear Daddy,
>   Here is the letter I promised to write to you. Basil uncle has come ... Anne has gone to America ... Lakshmi cook sends her regards ... Please tell me when you will be here ...

The writing is cramped, distorted; the phrasing Tamil-English, with the inversion (Basil uncle, Lakshmi cook). But it is coherent; he even wrote, on the back, his name and his address in Bangalore.

123

The next letter is from Madras, dated September 7.

> I am happy to be with Aggie and Patrick ... The weather
> is not too hot ... Daddy please come down as soon as you
> can in order that I can return to Bangalore and set up a
> house there for myself ...

On October 8:

> I have been to the pictures with Theresa, Lisa and Basil. I
> am taking Patrick and family out sometime soon ... The
> fuses which have been blown out by something that
> happened to me which [while] in Libya are shocks
> coming back again on being switched on to another
> system by means of a process which anyone will find
> difficult to comprehend ... It is with this thought in mind
> that I feel I can ask you to write to Patrick and Basil ... to
> help me to go to Bangalore where I will next start my
> great work ... with lots of love to Suyin.

Peter was so used to Bangalore where his childhood was
spent; he did not want to stay in Madras. His mother, Caro,
wrote to me:

> You must be getting news from Madras, consoling and
> relieving ... Both Basil and Patrick give me in detail
> Peter's condition and activities ... he seems ... improving
> under their kind care.

She thought Michael had been perhaps 'too harsh ... but no
doubt he felt it was good for Peter'.

Caro spent that Christmas and New Year in Madras,
staying with Theresa in her house, not far from Foreshore
Estate, and thus she often saw her son Peter. By 1981 her
health was deteriorating. Her relatives in Bangalore became
unable to care for her, and so she came to Madras again, to
stay definitively with Theresa and her husband Paul.

And here she was cared for, never alone. She joined in many of the family get-togethers, but in the end was too frail to do so, and remained for much of the time sitting in a rattan armchair on the verandah. Peter came to see her, but his shouting and pacing were at times too much for her. She was never alone, however, and died peacefully in her sleep in 1983. She was then eighty years old; she was thirteen years older than Vincent.

On October 27, 1981 Vincent received another letter from Peter:

I have not been very active which am being an invalid ... please come down to Madras and Bangalore as I have to start working as soon as possible. Suyin can come with you ... Right now I have returned from a bus ride down the Marina and back with Patrick for company, and am now celebrating our victory with Remy Martin brandy which is yours from the cupboard where it is kept. We went to Theresa's place for dinner. Chicken and macaroni. My stomach was almost okay. Every Sunday at 11 o'clock I speak to Patricia in Bombay.

And so we come to the end of a period in my life which neither I nor anyone connected with me will forget.

A very clear letter. His first bus ride. His speaking on the telephone to his sister in Bombay. Peter seems to be conscious of it for he adds a postscript:

P.S. Please excuse the writing in which is the longest letter I have written for almost 3 years ...

In November of that year he wrote two letters to me, thanking me for mine.

Please ask Daddy to come to India at the earliest ... Your sickly stepson.

And again:

> I am not fully recovered as I am taking medicine and the
> writing is not very good. I will be o.k in one week's
> time ... ask Daddy to come ... Please tell Daddy that I am
> not angry with Michael ...

Peter greatly wanted his father and his brother to get over
the friction which had taken place the previous year, on
account of him. He also did want to go back to
Bangalore – 'All my friends are there' – even though,
within six months, he grew accustomed to the Madras
environment. He was always involved in something: Basil
and Benny and Theresa taking turns to keep him interested.
Parties, dinners, walks. But he pleaded at first, almost
desperately, to have 'Daddy' with him all the time, to
return to Bangalore 'and a house of my own'. As time went
by, these demands became less strenuous; and, as Patrick
wrote: 'He realizes he has to be staying in Madras for a
while.' Peter wrote to me again:

> Your last letter reached me 4 days ago ... it must be very
> tough for you ... I am in the doldrums at the moment ... I
> was at the doctor's place this afternoon.

He then enclosed a Christmas card.

Vincent stayed that Christmas and New Year of 1980
with me in Switzerland, though he left immediately after. I
had insisted on it. 'You must not rush to Peter as soon as he
asks for you. Give Patrick and Aggie a chance.'

Every end of year I would receive some letter from Peter:

> Please allow Daddy to come for New Year to Madras and
> to Bangalore ... I promise never again to ask him to be
> sent at my bidding. The books for me have not arrived
> yet ... I intend keeping all your books in a set in my
> house ... which will be in Bangalore.

126

And on another occasion:

> You have been very good to me...please accept my
> thanks, with lots of love and warmth.

He wrote; and in 1983 he would start typing. Wrote to
friends of his, schoolmates who had invited him to parties
in their homes and been invited back by Vincent, when
Peter was in Bangalore. Now he told his father: 'All the
girls I knew are married, Daddy. What shall I do?' He said
the same to me, several times, as we met through the years
and on my passages through India to see him, on my way to
China.

'You get well first, and then you'll find a girl friend,' I
would say, somewhat inadequately. And he knew it, for he
would shake his head, and pace away abruptly, his face
sombre, shaking his right hand or holding it up in the air as
he always does when he is upset, in a turmoil.

He also wrote a letter to the mother of Y., the Belgian girl
he had known. And he wrote it in French, but with German
words interspersed:

> Ici est der jeune homme...Maintenant je suis tout
> seul...je voudrais participer dans the wellbeing de Y
> si possible. C'est tout pour l'instant. Excusez-moi
> pour le pauvre francais parceque je suis proficient en
> anglais.

A remarkable, coherent letter; offering to care for his
erstwhile girl friend. All this without prompting.

But the best chart of Peter's progress during those five
years from 1980 to 1985 is Patrick's letters. Faithfully,
indefatigably, every ten days, Patrick wrote in detail of
Peter's doings – the visits to the doctor, the psychologist,
the medicines prescribed, the outings, the food, the
'accidents'.

127

28 Jan. 81:
   Peter has accepted the fact he has to stay with us some time.
   Aggie and I will look after Peter with all the love and care that's in us.

There follows a long list of relatives 'drafted to look in turn after Peter, keeping him company, listening and talking to him ... listening to music from his cassette player. He speaks with none of the slurring and hesitation that marked his speech [previously].'

Peter has written a few letters to his former office [company A.C.E.C] in Belgium and is waiting eagerly for their replies.

At Christmas:

Peter went out of the house to invite a group of carol singers – they came [into the house] and sang ...

Throughout 1981 the record continues, Patrick remarks that 'on full moon days/nights Peter becomes restless. He tries to leave the house.' These attempts at nocturnal perambulations continued for several months.
   Now a typewriter was bought for him, and Peter began to type (at Patrick's suggestion).
   There was, in Madras, a round of birthday parties, and Peter went to all of them, each minutely reported by Patrick, including the special food – 'bland mutton stew, not to upset his stomach' – prepared for Peter.

November ... he went to a movie ... he went for a short cycle ride. Are you surprised, as we were? I accompanied him, of course, but the idea came from him ... his balance and coordination have not been affected ...
   He sometimes feels depressed ... thinking of his past ... He laughs more often, sings.

128

Then, on a 'not so good' day:

> Peter alternates between periods of sleepiness and
> sleeplessness; [when he is sleepy] we wake him up for his
> meals and try to interest him in doing something ... when
> sleepless he has to be restrained from exhausting himself
> by his incessant walking and talking ... the first two
> occasions were rather frightening ... I had no idea what to
> do ... now I know and I divert his attention.
>
> Peter went to see *Goldfinger* – Benny went with him.
> He dirtied himself 4 times today, but nothing to worry
> about, the stools were not watery.
>
> You'll be happy to hear that Peter, on his own initia-
> tive, has started going for bus rides, sometimes in the
> morning, another in the evening, but always with
> somebody. Simon [another relative] has been drafted for
> keeping Peter company.
>
> I manage to cope with the problems if and when they
> come up; please Vincent, don't worry ...

It seems that Michael and Anne (the latter back from a trip
to her relatives in America) came to Madras to see Peter.

> It has rekindled in Peter the idea of going to Bangalore,
> but ... Basil and I ... made it clear that it would be only
> after your coming ... so emphatic were we that he spoke
> to Michael: 'I'm sorry, Michael, I can't come to
> Bangalore without Daddy's permission.'
>
> A few days ago Peter played a few shots of table
> tennis ... he gave up – the table had too many faults.
>
> A game of chess, the moves of which he taught me, but
> we couldn't finish the course.
>
> We crack a few jokes, make him laugh; he said he
> hadn't laughed as hard since he came back from
> Europe ...
>
> He ... told us ... his ambition of entering politics.

In 1981, Vincent spent several months in India. During

those months there are no letters from Patrick; the letters only come, regular as clockwork, when Vincent is with me.

On May 14, 1981 Patrick wrote that Peter suddenly got all excited and exhorted us to 'leave this bloody country'. (It seemed Peter had been reading the newspapers, and was distressed by reading tales of woe and misery.)

It was at this time that Patrick also reported a small incident which happened in the doctor's clinic:

Peter voluntarily began talking about his aversion to X ... and Y ... [two relatives by marriage] who he said had tried to bugger him ... but then immediately started talking of what happened when he was 12 years old. We said X and Y could not have had anything to do with him [they were unknown to him at the time, and in another city] so he said they *looked* like the men who had tried.

In August 1981 Peter spent every Tuesday with his mother, and also took guitar lessons, Tamil lessons, and Yoga. But these did not last very long. In fact, until today, Peter's total inability (or refusal) to pursue any activity after a short while has not changed. Lack of concentration? A feeling that everything is useless? 'He puts any suggestion to work, to do anything, off... "I'll do it tomorrow," ' Patrick wrote.

Through Thomas's increasing disability (and a bout of malaria); through heat, servants coming and abruptly leaving, electricity cuts, illnesses; through all these years Patrick goes on, and on, reporting, minutely, on Peter:

September 81:
We are now letting him go out alone, as you suggested. He walks by himself... no more bodyguard ... The other evening, wanting to send a telegram to his old friend Mumtaj's wedding, he went by himself to the telegraph office – I was following – he had no knowledge of it, he

130

sent his message and came back; this is a big step forward...

In 1984, Peter was allowed more money by his father. He now went out, always accompanied, on buses, but towards the end of the year began to circulate on them by himself. He went on longer trips – on pilgrimages, to festivals, with Patrick and Aggie; the latter always took Thomas with them, and now they had to carry him. Thomas was always propped up with cushions, especially when he watched cricket on television. Cricket was Thomas's passion; and he would read books on cricketers, and on their scores, and follow every match. Vincent also took Peter on several trips to Bombay to see his sister Patricia who was working there as a medical doctor (doing family planning) for Tata industries. And once he brought Peter to meet me as I landed in Bombay, to spend as usual a few days in India with him (and, of course, to see some of the Family if possible), and then to continue alone to China. This meeting in Bombay with me was a small catastrophe. Peter reacts to me with more excitement, more shouting frenzy, than to any other member of the Family. I had arrived exhausted, the plane having been ten hours late. I was once again in the middle of some research for another book. Vincent had been away for nearly two months with Peter... in short, my temper was not the best. With a big smile Vincent greeted me as I tottered out of the airport with my luggage (no trolley, as usual). And I guessed. 'Oh Heaven, he's brought Peter to Bombay.' The smile gave him away. It was too broad.

Still with a lingering smile on his face, Vincent waited till we were in the taxi to take us from the airport to the hotel and said: 'Guess what? Peter's here. He wanted to see you.'

I started shouting, almost as badly childish as Peter. 'Nineteen hours on a plane, and you haven't seen me for eight weeks, and you bring your son to keep us company. That's great. Terrific. I'm leaving tomorrow, remember,

131

for China.' I said much more. I said how hard I worked, how much of him I'd given up, to fit in with our constant comings and goings, to keep everything running. Now I needed sleep, sleep, for a few hours.

And I would not get any sleep. For Peter indeed started shouting, gesticulating, as soon as he glimpsed me, and when he was brought back to his room by Basil and Vincent it was morning, and within an hour he was back, banging at my door.

'But he's so much better,' said Vincent, very subdued now. 'I wanted to show you how much better he was ... he's not like that, usually.'

'But he's like that with me,' I said hoarsely. I wanted to say: Peter is sexually deprived. He is thirty-eight years old. He's been living like a monk for four years. And he's got a fixation on me. Not entirely sexual (no, because he also makes advances to other women), but he reacts to me in an emotional way because he remembers our walks in Paris, he remembers our talks. I am a person he wants to be with ...

But I was too tired to say all this. I closed my eyes and felt very full of pity for myself. 'Did you ever think,' I said, 'that perhaps I too need sometimes a little care, a little pampering. A little vacation from Peter Peter Peter?' Even when we were together, in Lausanne, I knew that Vincent was thinking of Peter.

Of course, after a shower and sleep, I caught my plane and began to laugh. I should not have lost my temper. Vincent only wanted to show me how Peter had improved. He had not counted on this reaction. Peter had behaved so well, said Vincent, he'd so much wanted to see me ...

'After all, I'm tough. I'll survive.'

Over the five years Peter's letters to his father improved, both the typewritten ones and those he wrote by hand. However, even as late as June 1985, there would be noticeable lapses. In the following letter, Peter is upset – as a result, the writing has shifted back to what it was two years previously:

132

Dear Daddy,
   Sandya [a friend's daughter] has got Leukemia ... and I
met her father only last month, he seemed quite cheerful.
   Daddy I know you had an operation for your heart
some months ago ...

Vincent had, indeed, had an angioplasty in February 1985 at
the Mount Sinai hospital in New York. I do not think the
92-per-cent-blockage of his left coronary artery – dispelled
by this marvellous operation which supersedes, in some
cases, the better known bypass surgery – was entirely due
to stress over Peter; one of Vincent's brothers died of an
infarct at only fifty-five, and Vincent's doctor has been
watching his cardiac condition for some fifteen years. The
result of the angioplasty was satisfactory. But now it forced
us to reconsider. Who would look after Peter when Vincent
would no longer be able to do so? Patrick, of course. Patrick
and Aggie. 'We'll always do all we can,' said Patrick to me.
But decisions would have to be taken. Perhaps, in the end, I
would be the one to make decisions for Peter ...
   In January 1985 we had received two typed letters, quite
remarkably well typed, without any spelling mistakes,
addressed to Vincent and to me:

   This is going to be a very serious letter to which I would
   like a lot of replies. I would like to ask you have you done
   anything for Dorai? [Dorai was another member of the
   family, who was now suffering from depression.] You
   know, Daddy, yours is a very close and incestuous
   family, and I am very sure that you are all going to Hell,
   by which I mean that you are all very very bad. Except
   for Rina, Basil and me, I know that you are all going to
   the place without any lights; you are very lucky to be
   away from all these internecine family squabbles, and to
   act as the gracious Lord of all he surveys, because I can tell
   you that Suyin is very very good to you.
      You know, Daddy, Suyin is very careless when it

comes to dealing with money... You know, Daddy, Patrick has refused to take payments from me. I am very concerned, and wish to know how much you are paying Patrick and where this money is coming from.

Concern about money, living expenses for himself, had begun by 1984; and though he still had fits of generosity, he was now counting carefully the rupees in his pocket. No longer did he go round, as he had done at first, giving handfuls of rupees to the beggars he met.

In 1985 Peter's typed letters became more frequent; but, as a result, I find that his writing deteriorated; reverting to something like it was in 1980. Was this relapse muscular? Writing and typing are two very different skills. Did Peter exhibit a regression in some of the fine movements of the hand? His right hand was still affected with spasmodic movements, and now he would hold three fingers in a hyper-extended position, slanting backwards.

October 1984. There are intimate letters to his father; where he expresses very clearly the ambivalence of the child:

I wish you all the best, and of course Suyin too, who I don't think reads all your mail, though I still want to marry her. You are a cagey hermaphrodite.

Vincent laughs, immensely pleased with Peter's extending vocabulary.

January 29, 1985:

Daddy, I must first ask you why I was born? I mean, apart from all the bullshit about the holy spirit ... Can I ask you what you think about? I mean when you are thinking and not hallucinating, as I think you are doing most of the time?

I must first ask you Daddy to close your eyes, because I am going to propose to Suyin. Daddy, I must first ask

134

you to grant her a divorce, because you know she and I are going to get married. Or even if we are not going to get married, we are going to live in Sin. [A big S – a touch of Peter's quirky humour.]

And to me:

Suyin, I am sure you can make a very good wife to me, and am very worried that Daddy will not give you a divorce. You know that I am not joking.

I am very confident that nothing of my experience in Iran is ever going to come back to me, because it is all still as blank as it was from the moment I can remember that I was in hospital ... in Switzerland.

Peter's proposals of marriage are not confined to me. He proposes to a lot of the women he meets. We are not perturbed, knowing it is part of his natural estate; the release from a superbrain control, from the silencing agent of the 'normal' adult. We all know Peter tells the truth; he is not inhibited, and shouts at us the unpleasant things we would like to forget...

In early 1985 he proposed to several women and girls he met. For a while, he sang outside the windows of a neighbour in Foreshore Estate, whose pretty daughter attracted him. This could have led to very serious trouble; in India, irate fathers have been wont to take much offence, and vigorous action, against even an insistent look towards their females (wife or offspring). Even Patrick, when one of his daughters went out twice with the same boy, decided to go to the young man's family and confront them with: 'What are your son's intentions?'

But Peter was 'not well'; everyone in the city of Madras knew it, every pedicab-driver and hawker, all the neighbours, all the bus- and taxi-drivers knew Peter. He was, therefore, hallowed, protected, and his lively concern for them, the return of his idealistic love for the poor, the exploited, made him a favourite among them. No one took advantage of him, and many called him brother; some even thought he was a Naxalite.

A very nice and pretty Englishwoman from Switzerland, employed at Air-India, went to Madras on a holiday and visited Peter, who fell in love with her and wrote to us: 'I am very much in love with her.'

The whole subject of Peter's sexuality is one which from time to time comes up in discussion. Especially as Peter becomes increasingly mobile. Peter 'escaped' once; going away on his own for several hours. And returned on his own. Later he told me: 'You know, I went to the prostitutes' streets ... I saw them ... '

'How did you know where they were, Peter?'

'Someone told me ... ' He turned an anguished face to me: 'I met one of them ... she was so young, so sweet, she could have been my sister ... I told her: "You are my sister." I gave her money ... I didn't ... '

'I know you didn't ... '

One relative suggested that the Family buy, in a village, a girl; who would then be Peter's sexual companion. Of course, she would be an untouchable. More and more of them, the earth people, pariahs, untouchables, in South India, are becoming landless and dispossessed as agriculture becomes mechanized. The last record, based on statistics of the newspaper *The Hindu*, is that the number of dispossessed has increased threefold since 1970, from 20 to 60 per cent of the total number of agricultural labourers. So they come to the cities, surround themselves with appalling, fetid slums, and beg, and die. It was always possible to find a girl, healthy, no disease, who would be quite happy ...

I was at first horrified by this idea; although, later, I understood that my reaction was perhaps out of context. In the Indian context, where the most degrading things occur, because of the enormous disparity between the wealthy and the poor, I was being unrealistic. But Vincent also was against the idea. 'These people are smart; they'll come and beat Peter up and take away the girl,' he said. Which was another unsentimental way of stating facts, of stating the deep unease simmering in India, where more than 200 million are condemned to such a way of life.

Now we feel that perhaps, perhaps, there will be, somewhere, a woman, perhaps a widow with no children, who would like to have Peter as her husband. After all, Peter is not badly off. The money he had saved while in Libya and Iran, and what his father will give him, is enough, in India, to keep him in comfort for the rest of his life.

And Peter knows it. He knows it even better now that Vincent has given him his own cheque book; now that he goes to the bank and cashes his own money. 'I had to start trusting him with his own money...' says Vincent. And Peter, since then, is far more careful with money, because he knows it is his own. 'Of course when he goes to the bank, he shouts at the clerks, he carries on, he interrogates all those who wait ... but everyone knows, and smiles ... no one takes offence.'

In 1985 Peter began to do his own accounts. He performs mathematical sums with great precision. Slide rule in hand, he is again the engineer.

He buys presents for all the family. He goes to the market and buys fresh vegetables, to help Aggie and Patrick. He goes to 'wish' happy birthday to friends and relatives. He knows all the roads, the buses; finds his way all over Madras, or Bangalore, by himself. He now wants to travel by train, all by himself – he resents still having to be accompanied on trains, on aeroplanes.

X

I feel as if I have tried to extract a long-festering thorn lodged in my big toe. I once did step upon a prickly plant, hidden in thick grass in Malaya. A tiny dagger sank into my naked foot; remained, visible as a grey dot; burrowed deeper, cosily; layers of skin began to cover it.

With a needle, I gouged, and levered; widening a hole around the thorn; which remained embedded. Finally, with a pair of eyebrow tweezers, I started lifting off bits of skin round it, and flesh, until it could be gripped and drawn out. But only half came out; the other half remained. Decades later I can still see it, a faint grey dot in my big toe.

In the same way writing about Peter has been a semi-exorcism; trying to lift out the constant smudge, the irritation, the apprehension about what is still to come. For he will be with us both, Vincent and me, to the end of our lives. We must plan for his life after we are both dead.

And this is where Peter is a continual reminder to me of all those who care for children who are handicapped, permanently damaged, grown-up mongoloids of forty or fifty ... the spastics I see walking, cheerfully, with their mothers, their faces so trustful, radiant.

I think of far worse cases; those children in coma; parents who, like Vincent, have spent hours, days, weeks, calling, calling to them, calling them back from death ...

The efforts expended by so many in the Family, relaying themselves round Peter, is something that must be recorded; as all acts of devotion must leave behind their trace, their encouragement to us all never to forget our own humanity.

A week before we fly to India on Christmas Day of 1985 the telephone rings. It is Patrick. His son, Thomas, died that day.

There had been a tornado, sweeping over Madras in late November, wrecking many of the hutments, flooding the low-lying land. Water came up almost to the level of the apartment's cement floor at Foreshore Estate, up the four cement steps raising the buildings above ground. During those days, Thomas caught a cold; could not cough up the sputum which accumulated in his lungs, his chest muscles having almost disappeared. Aggie fed him, spoonful by spoonful, and then on December 18 he started choking, and was very quickly dead.

When we arrived in Madras Patrick and Aggie were quiet, as usual; discreet in their sorrow. But Aggie could not sleep, and would often start weeping, silent tears wetting her cheeks, which she would wipe automatically with a corner of her sari. At the end Thomas had been able only to turn the pages of a small book (on cricket), and his father knew that he had, at the most, another year to live. No more.

I sat on the door-stoop with Patrick. The tornado had long since gone, and it was a bright, sunny Indian winter day, warm as spring in Europe. Everyone was at ease in the cool weather, and the thousands of strollers along the wide, white-gold beach sent their voices and laughter skimming through the air. Strewn along the seafront was the debris,

not of the tornado, but of 'operation beautification', undertaken by the municipal government of Madras city to clear
the beaches of fishermen and their boats. Broken logs from
the *catamarans* lay about with clusters of men trying to put
them together again, tying them up to re-form embarka-
tions. Women and children squatted on the sand, repairing
the fishing nets torn by the police. For armed police had
been sent to remove 600 *catamarans*, and an army of municipal workers had hauled them away, after breaking them
up to pile them into garbage lorries. This was done to
'preserve the beauty of the seashore'. The fishermen were
supposed to congregate six kilometres further away, at
places devoid of fish or prawns ... and the whole affair had
taken place right in the midst of the prawn season, when
twice as much money as usual is earned. Seven hundred and
eighty families were thus deprived of their livelihood.
There had been violence, of course, and tear-gas, and *lathi*
charges, and finally bullets used by the police to kill six
fishermen; also an orgy of looting and assault as the police
invaded the fishing villages a kilometre further down the
beach.

But, unexpectedly, the whole city felt this was an
outrage; 20,000 people demonstrated in the streets; and
even the Middle Income Group had come out in favour of
the fishermen. This was the first time that, irrespective of
caste or religion (fishermen are considered low caste), there
had been such manifest solidarity against police brutality.
The Supreme Court then decreed that the *catamarans* must
be returned to the fishermen. But many of them could not
be put together again. They are built of logs of albasia
wood, which grows inland, and it takes time for the logs to
dry, to be shaped, to be tied into new *catamarans*.

We sat in the benign sun, around us peace and beauty and
violence and death, looking at the slight, thin, sun-black
fishermen putting their nets and their boats together.
Despite the Supreme Court injunction that each family
must be paid 15,000 rupees in compensation, many of the

fishermen would be in debt for years to come, and the money would take a long time to reach them.

The black pye-dog which Peter had befriended came round the corner with Peter trailing behind it, talking to it. 'Here dog, dog come here dog ... ' The dog wagged its tail but walked away, not heeding Peter's call. Every day Peter bought some *chapatis* from a pedlar and fed the dog. Peter turned to us. 'You know, that dog is very very ... smart. When Thomas died, he followed us all the way, when everyone left the cemetery that dog didn't go away; he sat, looking at Thomas's grave ... ' Peter rushed off, still shouting to the dog, but after a few metres he would forget it and go to the bus stop, and take a bus for his usual long ride, a ride to the end of the bus route, and back. Riding a bus made him feel better; he would sometimes ride buses two, three times a day.

'Patrick, tell me, how could you, all these five years, be so patient, so good to Peter? You never lost your temper, never shouted at him ... how did you do it?'

Patrick blinked at me behind his round glasses. 'I don't know ... we just felt he needed to be talked to ... I could always bring him around when he was shouting, or thrashing about, by talking to him ... '

'Yes, but five years of it, with no let-up, and also with Thomas ... You remember when Theresa's son got married to a Hindu girl, and we all went to the Hindu temple on the mountain ... '

Memories. The previous summer. The Family had hired two buses. Some relatives had come by train. The bride's more wealthy relatives came by car. I had been in one of the buses, with around forty Family members, and I would not forget that ride because I was covered with giant urticaria at the time. Someone in the Family had garlanded me with a wreath of blossoms, and among the blossoms (gladioli and jasmine and roses) was also poison ivy. Within two hours I was itching, within a day covered with large red raised patches which lumped, coalesced, started weeping. I was having calcium and cortisone injections, but I did not want to miss the wedding even if it meant a 250-kilometre bus ride. And Thomas had come with us, carried by his father and mother; we had gone up to the temple on the mountain; spent the night in the bungalows hired by the Family. Thomas had not missed anything: the music, the procession of guests, the great fire burning in front of the newly wedded couple, the Brahmin priest, white loincloth round his waist, naked chest crossed by the sacred thread, directing the ceremony, and interrupting himself at times for me to take photographs. 'Madam, very few are those who can attend such a real Hindu marriage ceremony.' A very obliging man.

'Did you enjoy the wedding, Thomas?' I had asked.

'Oh yes, Auntie, oh yes, it was fine.' Thomas's huge brown eyes, huge because all the muscles in his face were wasting away, had glowed with happiness.

'Yes,' says Patrick, 'Thomas shared everything with us, we never kept him at home alone.'

Thomas's little mound of earth was in the newest row destined for the Family. The Catholic cemetery, at Quibble Island, is only some ten minutes away from Foreshore Estate. I went to Quibble Island to say hello to Thomas; and then from grave to grave, not missing Appa. And here too was Caro. The Family was, after all, a Catholic family, and she had been Vincent's wife. I wondered whether, when the time came, Vincent would lie by her side ... and would there be a place for me? Perhaps not, since I wanted to be cremated, and there was no place at Quibble Island for people who chose incineration ...

'Patrick, what did you find most difficult, in dealing with Peter?'

Patrick thinks, thinks back. 'I think it was his soiling himself ... but then, when he started improving, and now he goes a month without an accident ... ' This is Patrick's triumph, his success. That Peter is no longer soiling himself. 'Peter was so upset when Thomas died ... he ran to

Theresa, he ran to Cissy, he wanted to phone for the doctor ... he was crying.' And Patrick looks at the children of the other M.I.G. families, playing cricket on the empty ground which separates the various buildings of the estate. Across this ground also come goats, kneeling to crop the scant grass, and pye-dogs, and a cow or two from the Hindu scavenger slum not far away.

I ask a final question: 'Tell me, what gave you this patience, this strength?'

He blinks again, and then says, a little surprised: 'I don't know, but I think ... it was faith, yes ... my faith.' Catholic. Patrick is a true believer, unwavering.

The girls are being tested to see if they too carry that gene which may, in their male offspring, give rise to the same congenital defect as occurred in Thomas. If so, they will have to practise self-control, for the Pope, the Pope is coming to India, and he will not hear of any birth control methods except the safe period, and self-control.

'You're a saint, Patrick,' I say.

He laughs, then becomes alert. 'Time for Peter to take his pills, excuse me.' He goes off in search of Peter ...

A few days later Peter is saddened because his pye-dog has been caught by the dog-catcher, in the name of 'sanitation', and it and others like it have been destroyed. 'Why, why did they have to kill that dog?' shouts Peter. 'He liked me, he liked Thomas ... that dog was better than many people.' And Peter is upset, and a little excited, and then Patrick quietens him down.

We fly to Bangalore. Michael and his three sons, now tall adolescents, greet us at the airport. The Family has repaired the small rents in its fabric; all is well once again as it comes together, all is well and Peter is radiant and shouts: 'Michael, Michael, how are you, Michael.' He loves his brother, which does not prevent him from suddenly saying something very hurtful to Michael, as he does to all of us ... but this is something we all have to endure, from time to time, and since Vincent has decided that it merely shows how much better Peter is, we all put up with it. Then Peter turns to me: 'Suyin, when my Daddy comes to India to look after me, what do you do?'

'I work, Peter.'

Peter chortles, he says: 'I know you hate being alone, I know ... ' We walk together in the beautiful dusk of Bangalore. The light is magical, touching every tree-bark with gold, every stone with a ruby glow. An Indian sunset, enchanted splendour, and the crimson and gold veering to mauve and blue as we walk along the road of our top-class luxury residential district with its neat gardens and new houses. Each house is hedged by low walls; an iron barred gate leads into its garden and garage (for here almost everyone has a car). Behind each gate are dogs, many German shepherd dogs. Peter goes up to the gates and starts barking at the dogs. I drag him away.

'Don't do that, they'll jump and bite your nose off.'

'But they like me,' he says, and tells me how much he hates the expensive houses. 'They're glorified jails,' he continues.

'But you too live here,' I tell him, and he paces away quickly, again in turmoil.

Just behind the 'residential colony', as the area is called, is a slum. There is a slum behind every luxury hotel, every condominium. A sprawl of mud; huts made of all the debris one can find. In the middle of it a charred area. 'Slum clearance' has begun, the usual 'sanitation operation' by the police, who simply burn the huts. Here are perhaps 40,000 souls, living off the offal of the wealthy houses. One can smell the slum fifty metres away. One always smells them. Sweat and urine and many other odours, compounded. And Peter backs away, backs out. 'I want ... I want to do something ... ' He shakes his head. Perhaps he knows he never will do anything now.

'Well, Peter is much better,' says Vincent that night. In my room, on my bed, lies the beautiful *Ponadai*, a splendid shawl of scarlet silk shot through and through with gold thread. Real gold. It belonged to Appa; given to him by the State of Tamil Nadu when he received a high honour from the Indian government. In 1985 we commemorated the 100th anniversary of Appa's birth; the city of Madras will name a road after him.

The assembled Family gave me the *Ponadai*, presented by Theresa, the Eldest Daughter of Appa. I look at it, and think I have done so little, so little, and now I feel responsibility upon me. I feel the *Ponadai* is mantling me within the Family ... And Vincent says: 'Now that Peter is better, I won't have to be with him so much.' I know this is his way of saying: 'Now I shall be with you a little more.' Perhaps. Perhaps it will be so; perhaps truly in another two years, three years, or more, Peter will become entirely capable.

'Yes,' I say. 'Yes.' But I do not have Patrick's faith, Vincent's faith. I shall go on, in suspended belief. Meanwhile, I am the daughter-in-law of an Indian family, and therefore must share. Share as much as I am able to do.

It is this sharing of love, kindness, effort, which enriches us all, enriches me. I want to say how grateful I am for all I have learnt with and through Peter. He has taught me that what each one of us is was provoked by accidental thrust; that each of us could be a thousand other selves. We are what we are by collision with others, we achieve coherence through suppression of those other, aborted selves we might have been.

For what is normality? Round me, I see many people shackled with inhibitions, far more so than Peter is. Sometimes, especially when he needles us, or comes out with candour and laughter with something that makes us squirm, which the silencing agent of our minds would inhibit us from saying, I feel he is actually rendering us a service; telling all of us how fragile is the building of our ego; how much we need, at times, to lie to ourselves in order to keep on being ourselves.

What is normality? In any street of New York, Paris, at any time, one may meet madmen. Who kill, who take

145

drugs. In every society, today, madness lurks very near the surface. Some television programmes terrify me. So many dispense madness, horror, vileness – which is also a form of insanity – with such unctuous and persistent conviction that we emerge stained, shabbied.

More and more, as we face growing numbers of the mentally sick, partly mentally sick, we are deluged with words which are supposed to explain, to catalogue, the various ways in which our brains go into havoc: alienation, anguish, fear of success, paranoia, schizophrenia, depression. We must ask ourselves whether discrimination, segregation, isolation of disturbed human beings ... whether this is the right way to treat 'abnormalities'; especially as so many of us, at some time, teeter into 'abnormal' behaviour.

Perhaps we should consider, as some people in India do, that abnormal beings are 'touched by God' and His special children. Not only to be borne, but to become a source of spiritual enlargement; by depriving ourselves of them, by putting them away, perhaps we are depriving ourselves.

It seems to me that the computer, the robot, its creations with programmed barriers, are an expression of our desire for a kind of horrifying perfection – categorical, unperturbed, immortal.

And killing.

The Family will sit, talk, play rummy. Peter will suddenly start shouting. 'I don't have to work ... ' he will shout. He has bought a table, and is building an aeroplane. A child of forty-three. But even this he will give up, for his attention span is still very short. But I know some people deemed 'normal' whose attention span appears to me even shorter than Peter's, and who are employed in offices. A contingent of floating young people, going from one job to another, filling in here and there. Perhaps because they are stoned on marijuana early in the morning, and all through the day.

'Come on, Peter, you said you'd finish building this plane last week ... '

146

'I'll finish it tomorrow.'

Tomorrow. He, at least, says tomorrow. Patrick says: 'He is bored ... he was disappointed with his last trip to Bangalore ... He would not be so bored if he had something to do.'

But how can we persuade Peter to *do* something, when he is not the kind of person who creates work for himself? For the essence of being unbored (with work or without) is to create, within the framework of routine, something new, surprising, original. His psychiatrist, his doctor, his father, urge Peter to 'find some work to do'. But of course, in a society where there are servants, where everything is done for him, how can he 'work'? I just long to make him dust every book of mine, as he once did ... that would perhaps be the best way of unclenching his mind, of a liaison between body and mind. I would like to have him help me with housework, at least wash one of his own shirts ... but in India, in the Family, this is unthinkable. There are laundry-men ...

'I'll be a great man, one day ... '

'I'm going to be the greatest ... '

Peter is still much afraid of failure. But he is finding out that the Bangalore of his dreams is fading, faded, gone. All his friends are men in their forties and fifties, with wives, children, grandchildren sometimes. All the girls he knew have married.

Peter has been left behind.

I'll take him out, just he and I, to the museum, to the park ... we'll talk ...

I am the daughter-in-law of an Indian family; I have my share of loving, my share of responsibility.

And with this share of loving I am blessed; for Vincent would not be the man he is, did he not leave me, at times, many times, for his son, who needs him. And I would not be the woman I am, did I not also, for all the love he gives me, accept to be, at times, very lonely.

147